THE TRIUMPH OF LORD PALMERSTON

THE TRIUMPH OF LORD PALMERSTON

A STUDY OF PUBLIC OPINION IN ENGLAND BEFORE THE CRIMEAN WAR

BY

B. KINGSLEY MARTIN

LATE DONALDSON BYE-FELLOW, MAGDALENE COLLEGE,
CAMBRIDGE

LONDON: GEORGE ALLEN & UNWIN LTD.
RUSKIN HOUSE, 40 MUSEUM STREET, W.C. 1

First published in 1924

Printed in Great Britain by
UNWIN BROTHERS, LIMITED, THE GRESHAM PRESS, LONDON AND WOKING

TO
MY FATHER

" Under free institutions it is necessary occasionally to defer to the opinions of other people ; and as other people are obviously in the wrong, this is a great hindrance to the improvement of our political system and the progress of our species."

WALTER BAGEHOT.

PREFACE

THIS essay is a study of the interaction between Government and Public Opinion during the period preceding the Crimean War. In writing it I have received encouragement, criticism, and suggestions from many friends. I want especially to thank Mr. G. Lowes Dickinson, of King's College, Cambridge, Professor Graham Wallas and Mr. H. J. Laski, of the London School of Economics, Professor R. Clifton Hall, of Princeton University, U.S.A., Mr. F. A. Simpson, of Trinity College, Cambridge, Mr. H. W. V. Temperley, of Peterhouse, Cambridge, and Mr. Reginald Harris, of All Souls College, Oxford—for help at various stages in its production.

For permission to publish new selections from the privately printed letters of the fourth Earl of Aberdeen I am indebted to the Marquess of Aberdeen, and I wish to thank both him and Lord Stanmore for their kindness in assisting me to make use of this correspondence.

I have also to acknowledge the gracious permission of His Majesty the King to use certain unpublished letters of Queen Victoria.

The substance of the section dealing with the mysterious resignation of Lord Palmerston in 1853 has already appeared in the first number of *The Cambridge Historical Journal* though I have, in one important respect, modified the conclusions I drew there, as a result of evidence of which I was ignorant, and to which Mr. Lytton Strachey was kind enough to draw my attention.

That I had the leisure to write this book is due to my good fortune in holding the Donaldson Bye-Fellowship at Magdalene College, Cambridge, and also the Procter Visiting Fellowship by which the University of Princeton gives an English student a rare opportunity of combining research with the study of American institutions in delightful surroundings.

Authority for every important statement of fact will be found in the footnotes. A bibliography at the end gives a list of my sources of information and the full titles of works to which reference is made.

B. K. M.

Cambridge,
January 1924.

CONTENTS

CONTENTS

CHAPTER VIII

THE EVE OF WAR (January–March 1854)

The Triumph of Lord Palmerston

CHAPTER I

INTRODUCTORY

OF all the unexamined assumptions of democracy none seems so strange to-day as the belief that public opinion is a reliable guide for a political society. Yet during the nineteenth century books dealing with politics usually postulated its existence and seldom questioned its reliability. Statesmen, too, proclaimed their " trust in the people " without specifying either to what people they referred or in what particulars they were to be considered worthy of trust. Indeed, they could do no other, since on that faith rested the whole theory of democracy. If public opinion was not infallible or at any rate commonly right, society itself was unsafe. No age can afford to question its fundamental assumptions. For doubt inhibits action and a prosperous age is necessarily a self-confident one. When the prosperity is at an end and the political structure has no longer the appearance of stability, the curious may find it instructive and even amusing to make inquiries which would formerly have seemed unnecessary or indiscreet.

The assumption was a natural one. The problem before democratic theorists, when their criticisms of eighteenth-century despotism were accepted, was to transfer the power surrendered by monarchs to a sovereign body consisting of millions of ill-informed persons. Rousseau was content to accept the infallibility of the " general will " of the inhabitants of a city State : his disciples had no doubt that what was true of Geneva was also true of a nation. Jefferson was sure that the small land-owning farmer at any rate would always be endowed with an inspired sagacity. " Those who labor in the earth," he wrote, " are the chosen people of God, if ever He had a chosen people, whose breasts He has made His peculiar deposit for substantial and genuine virtue. It is the focus in which He keeps alive that sacred fire, which otherwise might escape from the face of the earth."[1] But since practice demanded it, the assumption was made that this sacred fire existed among the whole people. The difficulty of enlarging a vision, naturally adapted to the needs of Main Street, to those of State or Federal politics seemed easily surmounted by the introduction of the newspaper Press. " Were it left to him," said Jefferson, " to decide whether they should have a Government without newspapers or newspapers without a Government, he should not hesitate a moment to prefer the latter."[2] In the same way, Jeremy Bentham, though not a mystic or a farmer, was enabled by a courageous belief in the human reason to reach a conclusion scarcely less optimistic. He prophesied that when the Press should be freed from the legal restrictions which fettered its natural development, the editor of a prominent newspaper would become the " President of a Public Opinion Tribunal," to which all politicians and public servants would

[1] Quoted by W. Lippmann, "Public Opinion," 268.
[2] Jefferson, xviii. 1.

be forced to render account. Of public opinion he writes: "Able rulers lead it; prudent rulers lead or follow it; foolish leaders disregard it. Even at the present stage in the career of civilization its dictates coincide, on most points, with those of the *greatest happiness principle*; on some, however, it still deviates from them; but, as its deviations have all along been less and less numerous, and less wide, sooner or later they will cease to be discernible; aberration will vanish, coincidence will be complete." [1]

The stumbling-blocks which Bentham saw in the way of this happy conclusion have been removed: the "taxes on knowledge" have been repealed and the franchise granted to a public presumably enlightened by the daily newspaper and a standard education. But the school book and the newspaper have not proved equal to the task which Bentham set them. The newspaper has always depended upon the public: it must please its readers, and truth, even when obtainable, is not always pleasing. A true judgment upon a political situation demands a willingness to accept unpleasant facts and to criticize not only one's opponents, but also oneself. Education has not so far been directed to either of these ends; it has taught men to read but not to criticize: it has imparted knowledge but not training in the conscious control of mental processes. The most highly educated persons frequently behave in an instinctive rather than a rational manner in regard to political matters. The physicist applies a critical method to physics and the economist to economics, but it is exceptional for either to adopt a scientific attitude to politics. Men look to the papers for what they want rather than for what

[1] Bentham, ix. 158, " Public Opinion Tribunal."

2

is true, and this alone would be sufficient to prevent the Press occupying the position which the early democrats claimed for it.

Even in the latter half of the nineteenth century, when journalism was a profession and news was not a marketable commodity, the Press could only express the existing opinions of political groups; it could never serve its nominal purpose of creating a rational public opinion.

Inadequate methods of education, however, are not the most important obstacle in the way of obtaining that coincidence between public opinion and the greatest happiness principle for which Bentham hoped. There is a more fundamental consideration. Since Bentham wrote, the size of the civilized world has immensely increased : the minds of men have not correspondingly enlarged. For in the world society of to-day men are conscious of an outside environment over which they have influence without direct contact. They are required to express opinions and to vote upon issues which will affect the lives of people whom they have never seen and cannot understand. The vast majority of political judgments are not based upon direct knowledge of facts but on second-hand information, itself the result of faulty observation. The combination of this new information with the contents of their minds at the time of its reception forms a picture upon which they act. How far men would act rationally if this picture corresponded to reality we do not know. Milton, indeed, asked if anyone had ever known " Truth put to the worse in a free and open encounter ? " At any rate, she has no chance of success until she is brought into the open.

" In putting together our public opinions," says Mr. Lippmann, " not only do we have to picture

more space than we can see with our eyes, and
more time than we can feel, but we have to des-
cribe and judge more people, more actions, more
things than we can ever count or vividly imagine.
We have to summarize and generalize. We have
to pick samples, and treat them as typical." Moreover, as we already possess a standard morality
and conventional idea of what the world is like,
the new facts must somehow be forced, with as
little readjustment as possible, into our accepted
picture. Thus a public opinion is not a moral
judgment on a group of facts, but a " moralized
and codified version of the facts." ¹ And as
standards and conventions vary among groups so
the picture varies, and the world is full of kindly
people cutting each other's throats under a misapprehension. They imagine that their opponents
see the things which they see and yet perversely
wish to support the wrong side. In reality they see
different pictures and therefore wish to adopt different
policies. It is uncommon for people to disagree
about a public question because there is seldom
any initial agreement as to what the question is.

The merits of the French Revolution, for instance, were never debated by the followers of
Burke and the followers of Tom Paine. They
were not arguing about the same thing. Burke
saw a great civilization, the product of a long and
glorious tradition, overthrown by a mob of ignorant
and ferocious *sansculottes*. He saw a beautiful
queen and a noble king foully put to death to
satisfy the passions of the base. Into this initial
picture the facts of the Revolution adjusted themselves. To Tom Paine this was " to pity the
plumage and forget the dying bird." He saw a
courageous people throwing off the shackles of

¹ Op. cit., 125.

tyranny, and entering into the heritage of freedom of which their rulers had wickedly deprived them. With this as a background almost any act of the Revolutionaries appeared in a favourable light. Here there could be no real discussion, because although the words used were the same, their connotation and associations were different. Each behaved disinterestedly in view of the situation as he saw it. But a warm heart is not a substitute for a knowledge of the facts.

This curious irrelevance in political discussion constantly exists between those who have direct knowledge and contact with events, and the outside public, whose picture of the situation depends on a dramatic representation of it in the newspapers. Statesmen, unlike political theorists, have always been conscious of this difference. For the function of a party leader in a democratic country is to persuade people that his method of dealing with the situation is the desirable one. He does not, usually cannot, do this by explaining the reason for his policy. He uses other and simpler means. Commonly he relies on the force of his personality. When he speaks of policy at all he uses symbols which can be easily adapted to the accepted picture of the situation. If possible, he will work in co-operation with the Press, which constitutes the other great source of popular symbolism. Sometimes his use of a section of the Press is conscious ; more often he establishes a popularity which the newspapers cannot ignore. Whatever his method, every successful statesman in a democratic country is constantly engaged in refreshing and recolouring the popular picture of himself and of the situation with which he is dealing. The degree to which statesmen have accepted their own symbols has varied. Some

have consciously acted their part : others have
instinctively been members of their own audience.
During the nineteenth century the most popular
statesmen were the least critical, and whether
the twentieth-century historian dubs them hypo-
crites or idealists depends on his natural turn
for hero-worship or iconoclasm. " The high
tragedians, who once ranted in the Parliaments
of the world, continued it at supper afterwards."[1]
But in the twentieth century, the discovery of the
power to be gained by creating popular images
has brought a new self-consciousness into politics,
and the most successful statesman to-day is the
one who believes in himself and trusts the people
while he is on the platform and believes in himself
and trusts nobody in the Council Chamber.

Under normal conditions there are many public
opinions competing and changing under constant
readjustment. But on one occasion there is only
one public opinion. When war is declared the
minority opinion is so small that it may be
neglected. The popular picture of the world is
set and vivid. There is an unanimous response.
A democratic nation never goes to war in the cold
mood of the " benevolent despot," and Voltaire's
representation of warfare is now as untrue as that
of Carlyle. The people enter war willingly, moved
by generous passion to revenge injustice or protect
the weak. The war must appear a battle between
right and might, and the enemy becomes the
personification of evil. As this regularly occurs
on both sides it is unlikely that it often represents
the situation accurately.

This essay attempts to analyse the development
of English public opinion on foreign affairs in the
years preceding the Crimean War. It is my object

[1] J. M. Keynes, *A Revision of the Treaty*, 4.

to discover how it happened that so large a proportion of the people of England came to possess a common image of a distant situation which made war seem the only honourable and generous policy.

There have not been many attempts to discover how such an image gains its place in the popular imagination. It has been simpler to adopt the attitude of the German Ambassador at Vienna in regard to the war of 1914 : " The original cause of the war," Dr. Naumann wrote, " could only be explained cosmically and metaphysically according to the philosophy of the individual. I believe that, with the most honest desire to attain to truth and lucidity, no other conclusion can be arrived at in the end. We set beneath our judicial decisions the words, ' By virtue of Right.' The more modest Turks write beneath theirs, 'Allah knows better.' In the present case, and least of all in the present case, shall we be able to find the Right ? We, too, must content ourselves by crying out : 'Allah knows better.' " [1]

The attitude of the modest Turks is no doubt the safest one for diplomats. But after a lapse of seventy years the historian may perhaps be allowed to leave, for a time at least, the cosmical and metaphysical explanations of a past war, even though he is warned that no other conclusion is possible. I have therefore ventured to examine contemporary evidence merely in the interests of truth and lucidity. Such an inquiry may at least throw light from a somewhat unusual angle upon the relationship which existed in the middle of the nineteenth century between facts, newspapers, politicians, and public. Perhaps Allah, knowing better, will forgive.

[1] Official German Documents relating to the World War, i. 56.

CHAPTER II

"A JUST BUT UNNECESSARY WAR"

1. The Problem.

In March 1854 the English Government declared war upon Russia. The Cabinet which took this step was perhaps as pacific as any that has ever held office in England. Moreover, the Prime Minister himself had formerly been on terms of cordial intimacy with the Tsar, while the majority of the Cabinet agreed with him in regarding Turkey, for whose " independence and integrity " many said we were fighting, as a crumbling relic of barbarism, whose existence in Christian Europe could not in any case long continue. For the rest, the Cabinet seemed to be divided upon every issue except the desirability of peace ; yet they were soon to be unanimous for war, and supported in their decision by their bitterest adversaries.

There can be no doubt, also, that the bulk of English political opinion was strongly in favour of war with Russia. This, perhaps, seems more strange when we remember that our ally against the Tsar was Napoleon III, with whom it had seemed, but a few months before, we were likely to enter into conflict. He had been execrated by almost every section of political opinion—by the Court as a " parvenu," by statesmen as an adventurer, by Conservatives as an exponent of the revolutionary nationalism of his uncle, by

Liberals and Radicals as the treacherous author of the *coup d'état*. Less than a year before he was believed to be on the point of invading England.

Finally, the Cabinet which had been for months negotiating for an alliance with Austria, upon which success against Russia depended, were in so great a hurry to declare war that they did so without waiting for Austria's pledge of support. Nor was this final breakdown of negotiations due to any clear issue on which agreement could not be reached. There was no deadlock. No vital question had arisen which diplomacy could not have settled if the temper of earlier discussions had been preserved. There was no immediate danger to the British Empire and, at first sight, no reason appears why war should have been declared in March 1854 rather than at almost any other moment during the preceding nine months. Further, the war itself did not bring its object any more clearly into light, for, as Mr. Strachey says, "its end seemed as difficult to account for as its beginning." [1]

Disraeli said that it was "a just but unnecessary war," and if justice consists in making war on monarchs who endanger peace, we must agree with him. For the one point on which there has been complete agreement among all parties is that the Tsar was rash and impolitic. There was much justification for the popular view that Nicholas was an undesirable person. Though no doubt wishing to extend his possessions in the south, there is every indication that he only intended to do so with the concurrence of England. He did not want war. He had shown, during the negotiations, an increasing willingness to abandon his earlier demands for the sake of peace. "It

[1] Strachey, 201.

can be truly said," writes Lord Stanmore, "that
the war was undertaken to resist an attack which
was never threatened and probably never contemplated." [1]

The origin of the Crimean War, therefore, has
always remained something of a mystery, and
historians have not found the lengthy diplomatic
correspondence which preceded it sufficient either
to explain its objects or to demonstrate its necessity. During the months in which a way of peace
was earnestly sought there were several occasions
when the negotiations were on the very point of
success : on each of these some unexpected event
occurred to prevent a settlement. "It seems,"
said Lord Aberdeen, "as if some fatal influence
must be at work." Strangely enough, the fatal
influence often proceeded from the negotiators
themselves. Could it really be that some malig-
nant demon was delighting not only in throwing
obstacles in the way of the peace of Europe, but
also in inspiring the peacemakers themselves with
the madness of Heracles so that they destroyed
their own offspring ?

Historians, looking for a more conventional explanation, have been led to single out for blame
one or other of the chief actors on the European
stage. The Tsar, the Sultan, Lord Aberdeen,
Lord Stratford de Redcliffe, Louis Napoleon, and
Lord Palmerston have all been condemned as the
authors of the war. But in no case has this creation
of a scapegoat been found sufficient in itself. In
the last resort, the case against the individual
breaks down, and the accused can cry out in
triumph to the peoples of Europe : "I did not
create the war : you wanted it. I was your
mouthpiece. Blame public opinion." "Whatever

[1] Stanmore, *Sidney Herbert*, i. 18[2].

influence Palmerston possessed," one authority tells us, " he owed partly to his knowledge of foreign affairs, but far more to his inborn sympathy with the nation. *It was they, not he or any other man, who really made the war.*" [1]

Thus the historian has learnt to use public opinion as the final mystery, and when the plot is too thickly entangled and the characters all seem mere puppets, helpless in the midst of great events, public opinion is discovered as the *deus ex machina*—mystic, impalpable, and unexplained. It has taken its place as the latest recruit in a long line of similar deities. " Economic necessity " no longer carries easy conviction, even " national character " is insufficient : no longer may we comfortably attribute man's backslidings to an all-wise Providence, nor adopt the equally simple expedient of Voltaire and summon " Chance " to cut the knot we fail to disentangle. Therefore, we personify public opinion.

Perhaps Kinglake best demonstrates this tendency to speak of the Public as a single individual whose ratiocinations explain the otherwise inexplicable ; but later historians of a less picturesque turn of mind have indulged the same weakness. We may take the incident of Sinope as an appropriate instance. On November 30, 1853, some Turkish ships were destroyed by a larger squadron of the Russian fleet. Russia and Turkey were formally at war, and the event was a normal naval disaster. Historians have for the most part agreed that it was this event which, for some unexplained reason, so excited opinion in England and France that peace became impossible. " But for the catastrophe of Sinope," writes Stanmore, " peace between England and Russia would have remained

[1] *Cam. Hist.*, ii. 381. (My italics.)

unbroken"; and he explains that its importance
lay in its effect on the public.[1] Kinglake declares
that when Englishmen came to know of the catastrophe of Sinope (under a misapprehension that it
was a "treacherous slaughter") "they were in-
flamed with a desire to execute justice," although
the "conscience of the nation was sound and
men were as well convinced as ever of the wicked-
ness of a war wrongfully or wantonly incurred."[2]
Sir Spencer Walpole tells us that: "Opinion in
neither capital stopped to inquire whether the
attack had been caused by the hostile action of
the Western Powers,"[3] and Mr. G. M. Trevelyan
remarks that the "British public *chose* to call
the affair the 'massacre of Sinope.'"[4]

Now these statements are not in themselves
untrue; they are merely the shorthand of everyday speech introduced into historical writing. They
represent not the misstatement of a problem,
but its evasion. For if, as is certainly the case,
public opinion was one of the most potent factors
in bringing about a European war, some sort of
analysis and inquiry into its nature is surely
essential. Public opinion, after all, does not declare
war, write dispatches, or mobilize troops: if
these things were done by its influence there must
have been channels through which it worked.

Public opinion is a collective term which can
only be accurately used to denote a common
opinion relative to some one defined issue held
by an effective majority in a certain group of
persons. Public opinion does not "do" anything; it either exists or it does not exist. It
exists in those cases where in a specified group
those who differ from the majority as to the advisa-

[1] Stanmore, *Aberdeen*, 228.   [2] Kinglake, ii. 61.
[3] *C.M.H.*, xi. 217.   [4] Trevelyan, G. M. 220. (My italics.)

bility of a certain action are so few or so ineffective as to be negligible.

Accordingly, in this essay, there are two problems before us. The first is to discover why there was for a few months an English public opinion in favour of war. How came it that the common indifference to foreign affairs disappeared and the usual variety of opinion became transformed into a single emotion directed towards the same object ?

There is a second question. In what way did the various conflicting views of the Eastern Question affect the course of diplomacy during the earlier negotiations ; and during the latter period, when it is accurate to speak of the existence of a public opinion in favour of war, by what machinery came it about that this voice of the people became the diplomatic voice of the State ? How was public opinion made effective ?

Before proceeding to the detailed answers of these questions it will be convenient to make a formal statement of the negotiations to which the latter part of the essay must constantly refer. Such an account, written primarily for purposes of reference, must be as short, clear, and colourless as its lengthy, complex, and controversial nature allows.

2. The Negotiations.
(March 1853–March 1854)

During the long negotiations which finally resulted in the Crimean War, the question at issue was the extent to which any European Power, or group of Powers, might exert influence over the policy and administration of Turkey. It was almost axiomatic among the diplomatists of Europe that internal dissensions would break up the Ottoman

Empire in the near future, unless it was supported from the outside. Politicians, therefore, discussed whether this outside support should be given in exchange for promises of reform on the part of the Sultan, or, whether, on the other hand, a partition of Turkey would be the most satisfactory method of settlement. The "integrity and independence of the Ottoman Empire" was a phrase chiefly reserved for public speeches. "No form of words could have been chosen more grotesquely inconsistent with the notorious facts of the case," wrote one member of the Aberdeen Cabinet. No statesman believed that Turkey could be free from foreign interference. The phrase, if it meant anything, suggested "that Turkey was so weak that her integrity and her dependence could exist, even nominally, only on condition of the European Powers agreeing to abstain from separate attacks, and of their acknowledging among themselves that this should be held a common and a binding obligation." [1]

From the Treaty of Kainardji in 1774 onwards, the internal administration of Turkey had been a matter of international agreements and of international rivalries. A series of conventions had dealt with the questions of the transit of the Dardanelles and the treatment of Christians in the Ottoman Empire. Diplomatists were under no delusion that these questions were finally settled, and when, in 1844, the Tsar visited England, he had discussed at length with Sir Robert Peel, the Duke of Wellington, and Lord Aberdeen, the probable dissolution of the Ottoman Empire and the need for Anglo-Russian agreement if it should be "foreseen that it must crumble to pieces." A secret Memorandum, embodying the result of these con-

[1] Argyll, i. 441.

another suggestion which Lord Stratford regarded as unjustifiable. He demanded for Russia a definite statement of her right to " protect " the Greek Christians in the Ottoman Empire. What exactly this " protection " meant it was, and still is, impossible to say. France exercised some kind of protectorate over the Catholics under Turkish rule : the Tsar declared that he only demanded a restatement of his rights, often admitted by treaty, to a similar protection over the Greek Christians.[1] But whereas the French protectorate affected only a few thousands, the Russian would affect almost as many millions. To the Western Powers this seemed to make the Russian demands dangerous and unjustifiable. Lord Stratford even declared that France could, with equal reason, demand a protectorate over British Catholic subjects in Ireland.[2] To the Tsar, on the other hand, the large number of Greek Christians under the Sultan's Government merely made his obligation to protect them the more obvious. There was, moreover, no doubt that by treaty he possessed some rights of protection : the question was how far these rights extended.

In May, Count Nesselrode wrote of " the fact of the sympathy and the community of interests which attach our population of fifty millions to the twelve millions and more which comprise the majority of the Sultan's subjects." " However

---

[1] Vide *E.P.*, i. 191–7, 243, and *Diplomatic Study*, i. 152. In this Russian apologetic it is claimed that Prince Menschikoff's demands " introduced no innovation ; they merely confirmed it by a new guarantee which the last infractions had proved to be necessary." Menschikoff was left to decide for himself " the extent to which the demands were to be pressed." Cp. *Cam. Hist.*, ii. 364.

[2] *E.P.*, i. 236.

distressing," he continued, "this fact may be to those whom our influence alarms, it is still not less a fact." [1]

The Porte, in accordance with Lord Stratford's advice, refused to admit any such Russian protectorate, and in May, Prince Menschikoff, whose behaviour had from the first been arrogant and insulting, after delivering his demands in the form of an ultimatum, left the Porte with much show of anger. This result was a diplomatic victory for Lord Stratford, and as such alone was intensely irritating to the Tsar. [2]

The meaning of the word " protectorate " and the extent of Russia's legal claims should have been matters for diplomatic discussion. Prince Menschikoff's behaviour had already made them a menace to peace, and, early in June, the Tsar proceeded to make the situation far more serious by dispatching troops across the Pruth into Waldachia and Moldavia. The Principalities were the property of Turkey, and it was only under certain unfulfilled conditions that Russia had the right to occupy them. [3] The Tsar now claimed that he was justified in holding the Principalities as guarantees (without any further hostilities) until Turkey should see fit to fulfil her treaty obligations. His action was both illegal and impolitic. Unfortunately, France and England had by this time also taken steps which, though less serious than that of the Tsar, were almost equally inimical to the cause of peace.

When Prince Menschikoff had first gone to Constantinople and had opened his negotiations

---

[1] *E.P.*, i. 244.

[2] Cp. *E.P.*, i. 230. Clarendon, as early as June 7th, admitted that it was Stratford's presence which prevented a settlement.

[3] By the Treaty of Adrianople in 1829 the Principalities were under Turkish sovereignty but were " guaranteed " by Russia.

by refusing to honour Fuad Effendi, the Turkish
Minister, Louis Napoleon had dispatched his fleet
to Salamis. This was the first threat offered by
either side, and the English Government was
" inclined to attribute this unwise proceeding to
the vanity of the French, their passion for doing
something, and above all the inexperience and
want of *savoir faire* in high matters of diplomacy
of the Emperor and his Ministers."[1] The Cabinet
therefore approved the action of Dundas, the
Chargé d'Affaires at Constantinople, who had refused Admiral Rose's request to be allowed to
co-operate with the French fleet in its first movement of hostility to Russia.[2]

But the British Government did not continue
this pacific policy, and early in June our fleet was
also dispatched to the entrance of the Dardanelles,
and Lord Stratford was empowered to call it to
Turkey's assistance in case of need. This event
took place at the very time that the Russian
troops were crossing the Pruth, and was not, as
Count Nesselrode suggested, the cause of the
Tsar's violation of Turkish territory.[3] It is equally
clear that our advance was not made in answer to
Russia's ; in fact, the actions were taken each in
anticipation of the other, and both made the
likelihood of a peaceful solution to a diplomatic
question less probable.

On the Russian side the invasion of the Principalities had the effect of bringing Austria and
Prussia into the quarrel and putting the Tsar in
the wrong, irrespective of the merits of his claims
upon Turkey : on the English and French side
the movement of our fleet involved us in a Turkish
quarrel, though the questions which directly affected
our interests there had been settled. The question

[1] Grev., vii. 54.   [2] E.P., i. 93.   [3] Ibid., i 346.

of peace and war now depended on concerted action by the allies, and the avoidance of any further movements which could prevent the diplomatic issue receiving the cool consideration of statesmen.

In July, therefore, the Four Powers (England, France, Austria, and Prussia) submitted to the Russian Government a Note which their representatives had drawn up at Vienna.[1] It was supposed by them to guarantee Russia's rights at the Porte while at the same time ensuring the Sultan's sovereignty. It was immediately accepted by the Tsar, and early in August the whole question seemed to be at an end.

Unfortunately, though drawn up on Turkey's behalf, the Note had not been submitted to Turkey, and the Porte, when asked to accept it, refused unless certain modifications were introduced. These modifications did not at first seem important. The Vienna Note had been diplomatically vague. Turkey wished to define certain points more clearly. Russia, by the Treaties of Kainardji and Adrianople, had a limited right of interference in certain specified provinces. Turkey insisted that Menschikoff's suggestion that " the Orthodox Church and clergy throughout the Sultan's dominions are to be secured in the possession of all the rights, privileges, and immunities which they have enjoyed *ab antiquo*," [2] could not be admitted. A clause of this sort would have seemed to justify the Tsar in regarding all specially conferred rights of protection as continuous, and liable to extension over all Greek Christians under the Sultan's rule, and not merely over those districts where any specific difficulty

[1] It had been preferred to a Note offered by Lord Stratford. *E.P.*, ii. 30.
[2] *E.P.*, i. 268.

had at first arisen. The Sultan denied the Tsar's
right to this universal protection, and therefore
suggested a few verbal alterations in the Vienna
Note which would make this distinction clear.
Unfortunately, the Tsar had accepted the Vienna
Note on condition that it remained exactly as it
was presented to him, and, perhaps naturally,
refused to accept modifications of terms which had
been presented to him as final. Moreover, he
believed that the modifications had been suggested
to the Porte by his opponent, Lord Stratford.
It was now an open question whether England
and France would support Turkey in her refusal
to accept the terms drawn up for her. There
seemed at one moment a probability that England
would recall Stratford and compel Turkey to
accept the Vienna Note in an unmodified form.
This solution of the difficulty was made impossible
by a singular accident. A private dispatch,
written by Count Nesselrode, found its way
into a Berlin paper. This dispatch showed that
the Vienna Note, according to the Russian interpretation, left her the right of intervention to
protect the Orthodox in Turkey. This the allies
had not intended explicitly to admit, and Turkey
therefore seemed justified in her demand for
modifications. In September, therefore, the
Vienna Note was reluctantly abandoned, and
the negotiations began once more from the
beginning.

The publication of Count Nesselrode's dispatch
had a further unfortunate effect : it prevented
the English Cabinet, much to Lord Aberdeen's
subsequent regret, from considering with due care
a counter-offer made by the Tsar. Immediately
after the abandonment of the Vienna Note the
Tsar paid a visit to Olmütz, where he met the

Austrian Emperor and gave a private interview to the English Ambassador, Lord Westmorland. The Tsar's manner was extremely conciliatory, and he offered, if the British Government would enforce the Vienna Note, to issue a declaration denying his right to the general interference feared by the Sultan.

In view of the fact that Nesselrode's dispatch had discredited the Vienna Note, it was probably now impossible to enforce its terms on Turkey, even when accompanied by such a declaration. But the Russian offer made it amply possible to reopen negotiations on the basis of the Tsar's declaration, and it was the failure to do this that Lord Aberdeen so bitterly regretted.[1]

Instead of responding to the Tsar's offer of conciliation, England took a further step towards actual hostilities. On September 23rd, news having reached England of disturbances at Constantinople, Stratford was ordered to send for the fleet to protect the Sultan from revolution and British subjects from loss of life and property.[2] This was a violation of the treaty of 1841, which declared the neutrality of the Dardanelles. Questioned by Baron Brunmow, Clarendon explained that Russia's violation of neutral territory across the Pruth had destroyed the sanctity of the treaty of 1841.[3] England was now definitely committed to the help of Turkey. There was still hope that negotiations would settle differences if hostilities could be prevented between Turkey and Russia. But by the beginning of October, Turkey was in a warlike mood, and, though pressed by the allies not to jeopardize the negotiations, an ultimatum was sent to the Tsar and, on his refusal to evacuate the Principalities, Turkey declared war. The neces-

[1] Vide below, 223.   [2] E.P., ii. 116.   [3] Ibid., ii. 126-7.

sary difficulties of diplomacy were now increased by the excitement of actual hostilities, and the presence of the fleet in the Dardanelles made it impossible for the Tsar to regard the allies as neutral mediators.

A number of different Notes were drawn up during the autumn of 1853, and one, composed by Lord Stratford, was eventually decided upon for presentation to the Tsar.[1] It is unlikely that any Note drafted by Stratford would have received the Tsar's approval, but by the time this final proposal reached St. Petersburg other outside events made its acceptance impossible.

The Tsar, therefore, dispatched a conciliatory ambassador, Count Orloff, to Vienna, with the double purpose, first of gaining Austria to his side in case of hostilities, and secondly of coming to terms with the allies if possible.[2] Before his return to Russia, Count Orloff made a suggestion which, if it had been examined on its merits, would have settled the whole dispute. He offered to present the gist of the allied terms as set forth in a protocol of January 13th to the Tsar, and to recommend him to send a Note from St. Petersburg embodying them. He also suggested that Dr. Meyendorff, the Russian Minister at Vienna, should be given authority to adopt any modifications which the Conference should deem necessary. This Note, when agreed upon by all the Powers, was to be sent to the Porte ; an armistice was to

---

[1] Vide below, 42. This note was signed December 5th, accepted by the Sultan, and reached the Tsar at the same time as the demand for him to withdraw his fleet. (Cabinet decision, December 22nd.)

[2] Stanmore is the only historian who has taken these final negotiations seriously, and he over-emphasizes their importance. Opinion at the Court and in the army at St. Petersburg was alone sufficient to make it difficult for the Tsar to avoid war at this last moment. Cp. *Cam. Hist.*, ii. 375.

follow its acceptance, and the immediate evacuation of the Principalities by Russia was to take place simultaneously with the withdrawal of the English and French fleets.[1]

At this point, if we had only the diplomatic correspondence to go by, there would seem no reason why a settlement should not have been immediately reached. Yet we find that when the messenger from St. Petersburg brought a draft, conceived substantially in accordance with Count Orloff's suggestion to Vienna, the allied representatives there had been in so great a hurry to end negotiations that they had already formulated an ultimatum and were on the point of dispatching it to the Tsar. An ultimatum demanding the immediate evacuation of other people's territory is, by a curious tradition of diplomacy, known to be equivalent to a declaration of war. The messenger was therefore " retained till Monday " in order that the Tsar's terms could be examined, and in this way " the reproach of having acted with precipitation " be avoided.[2] The new proposals were hastily examined and pronounced "inadmissible." They were declared by the Council to be a " snare, skilfully laid in order to produce division amongst us," [3] and the ultimatum proceeded on its way to St. Petersburg.

What, then, were the differences between the allied terms and the Tsar's proposals which made them inadmissible ? The principal differences were two : one was that the Tsar proposed to negotiate first and withdraw his troops from the Principalities when other questions had been settled,[4] and the second, that he wished to treat

---

[1] *E.P.*, vii. 39.   [2] Ibid., 70–2.   [3] Ibid., 72–80.

[4] The earlier withdrawal of his troops would have been impossible for the Tsar if only because of the excitement of the war party in St. Petersburg. Vide below, 160.

directly with Turkey as to the details of the treaty, and to arrange with her a place of meeting in Turkish or Russian territory. " There lay the insurmountable obstacle." [1]

It might have seemed that the diplomats at Vienna could have solved these questions without a recourse to arms. The truth was that the Conference had already decided upon war unless Russia should surrender unconditionally. It is curious that the one point of importance at issue between the allies and Russia—that of direct negotiation with Turkey—was not considered the reason for the termination of diplomatic relations. Lord Cowley declared that Count Orloff's terms were inadmissible, first because Russia was likely to attack Constantinople, and secondly, because discussion of them " would destroy the Union of the Four Powers." The terms, in fact, were not considered on their merits, and there is possibly some justice in the complaint of the Russian Government that " the Porte had been asked on what conditions it would consent to make peace. The Conference approved these conditions, and communicated them to us. Was it forbidden to us to examine them and to express our opinion ? Or was the Porte to be the sole arbiter in this debate ? " [2]

But if the object of this refusal to consider Russia's proposals was to ensure that the Four Powers should act together, the method adopted was singularly unfortunate. On the 23rd and

---

[1] *Diplomatic Study*, 43. " The evacuation of the Principalities (simultaneously with that of the Straits) was to be not the first point but the last. It was to be the consequence not the condition of peace. In the next place negotiations were to be absolutely direct, and were to take place either at St. Petersburg or Bucharest. There lay the insurmountable obstacle."

[2] *E.P.*, vii. 80.

24th of February, Clarendon telegraphed to Vienna and Berlin, asking whether Austria and Prussia would join with England and France in demanding the evacuation of the Principalities and, further, what their policy would be in the event of Russia's refusal.[1] Austria offered support to the ultimatum but did not pledge herself to a declaration of war, and Prussia cautiously replied that she " would not oppose " a demand for evacuation.[2] The ultimatum was immediately sent ; Russia refused compliance, but neither Austria nor Prussia joined England and France in the declaration of war which followed.

It is clear that we must look to events outside the diplomatic correspondence to account for the failure of the negotiations. War was begun not because a diplomatic deadlock had been reached, but because the negotiators had ceased to believe in the possibility of peace. The event which was primarily responsible for this change of attitude was the incident of Sinope. On November 30th a Turkish fleet, in defiance of the expressed wishes of the allies, had cruised in the Black Sea, and had been overtaken and destroyed by a larger Russian squadron.[3] It is difficult at first to see why this should have caused surprise : Turkey and Russia were officially at war, and though Russia had at first announced that she only held the Principalities as a guarantee and would commit no further aggression, she could claim that Turkey had already released her from this pledge by attacking the troops in the Principalities. But

[1] E.P., vii. 57.
[2] Ibid., 64. Cp. Letters, iii. 15–16.
[3] Stratford reported on November 5th that he had prevented the Turks from sending ships into the Black Sea : a fleet did, as a matter of fact, enter the Black Sea and part of it returned leaving the rest to be destroyed by the Russians.

the British fleet was within a few miles of the battle, and it was clear that our action in sending our fleet into the Dardanelles had really committed us to protect Turkey. The English and French fleets therefore " invited " the Russian fleet to withdraw into Sevastopol, and it was the news of this ultimatum which reached the Tsar at the same time as the Note drafted by Lord Stratford.[1] Under these circumstances the Tsar inquired whether Turkey's fleet was also to be asked to retire, and it was not until he discovered that it was only to Russia that the Black Sea was to be closed that he withdrew his ambassadors from Paris and London. He dispatched Count Orloff with a final offer of conciliation, but the excitement in Europe had, as we have seen, infected the negotiators themselves, and terms which would have been acceptable a few months earlier were now dismissed almost without consideration.

We have seen that these negotiations were complicated, and their success baulked by a series of movements of a threatening character. The Tsar's initial action in crossing the Pruth, the Sultan's premature declaration of war, the advance of the allied fleet first to the Archipelago, then to the Dardanelles, then up to Constantinople, and finally into the Black Sea—all these actions militated against the success of the negotiations ; while the request made to the Tsar to keep his fleet in the harbour of Sevastopol and the final hasty dispatch of the ultimatum were both actions which made war certain when peace was, as it seemed, in sight.

In England the Cabinet which was responsible for some of these contradictory actions was, for the most part, anxious for peace. Apparently it

[1] Vide above, 38. Cp. *Cam. Hist.*, ii. 373.

was not a free agent. It was compelled, we are told, by public opinion.

The analysis of this mysterious force involves the answer to three questions. First, we must ask what views contested the field in England concerning foreign affairs in general and the Eastern Question especially ? What public opinions existed concerning England's foreign policy ? And where there were no conscious " opinions," what associations had grown up round such names as Tsar, Napoleon, Palmerston, Aberdeen, Stratford, Dardanelles, Austria, France, Turkey, and Russia ? In this analysis we must carefully distinguish between those who were experts, at any rate in the sense that they had some first-hand knowledge of the diplomatic situation, and those, the great bulk of the nation, who relied entirely on indirect evidence.

Secondly, we must discover in what form new information on our foreign relationships came to this inexpert public. What, in fact, were the sources of public information ? This involves an examination of the newspapers of the period, the pamphlet and other literature devoted to foreign affairs, and the speeches in Parliament and at public meetings dealing with the Eastern Question. And here, heedless of journalistic etiquette, we must become eavesdroppers and hear what little we may of the conversations which discreetly pass in the Editor's room, and even probe that private correspondence which has always existed between those who govern and those who persuade the governed of their fitness to do so. We must even risk an opinion as to the motives for this persuasion and ask, since the art of journalism is one of selection, why the Editor emphasized this story and neglected that source of information. In other words, how did the facts become " news " ?

Thirdly, we must inquire what effect the news, as presented, had upon its readers ; what new pictures of the situation in the East were formed, and how these new popular images reacted upon the statesmen, who, though often supplied with better information, were in the last resort dependent on popular favour.

Though taking different views of the Eastern Question, the Cabinet members at first reached agreement without great difficulty, but, before the end of the period, the reaction of newspaper opinion led to the adoption of a policy disapproved of by the Premier and a number of his colleagues.   Meanwhile, the newspapers and periodicals, though at first taking widely different views, tended to present a similar picture of the situation.   To this image *The Times* almost alone among important papers refused to conform.

The second period, during which the Vienna Note seemed to offer a hopeful solution, found the Cabinet at first almost united.   But with the publication of Nesselrode's interpretation on the one hand, and on the other the discovery that Turkey was certainly more anxious for war than Russia, the division in the Cabinet became irreconcilable.   Outside, the papers, after a few days of confidence in the prospect of peace, became insistent in the demand for definite aid to Turkey. Russia's bad faith was now accepted as certain, and even *The Times* began to falter.

The third period, beginning in October, was marked by crowded meetings on behalf of Turkey which had just declared war on Russia, in spite of the warnings of our Government.   In the Cabinet the dissension had become intolerable, and Lord Palmerston resigned.   The news of this resignation followed hard upon the announcement that Russia had caught a small Turkish fleet and destroyed it almost within earshot of our protecting fleet. The required setting was now complete : a cruel Tsar, a trustful Turkey, betrayed by a faithless Government and a Court in secret alliance with Russia, and the one " English Minister " driven out by their machinations.

During the final period the newspapers had reached something approaching unanimity. Almost all the critical voices were hushed, and an increasing pressure was brought to bear on a Government which finally declared war, without the co-operation of one of our most important allies, at a time when a few days more patience might perhaps have procured peace.

The picture of the Eastern struggle, misty and diverse at first, has settled in hard and vivid outline. The subtleties and uncertainties which first made decision difficult have disappeared. In the minds of thousands is the same set of images, and the same reaction. Russia, as becomes a villain, is diabolic, clever, yet somehow easy to defeat by courage and a fleet ; Turkey, the distressed maiden, bravely bids the ravisher defiance ; the suggestion that England shall complete the romance in the rôle of the gallant knight-errant is overwhelming. The voices of honour and self-interest are indistinguishable ; there is the cruelty of Sinope to avenge, our trade and prestige in the East to protect. The opposition of Bright and his friends has become treachery, and even though the Tsar is perhaps willing to leave his bullying and flee before our wrath, Honour urges forward and Glory lies before.

CHAPTER III

LORD PALMERSTON AND PUBLIC OPINION

(1846 to 1852)

1. The Peace Society and the Policy of Non-intervention.

DURING the thirty years' peace which followed the Napoleonic Wars the vast majority of Englishmen were not interested in foreign affairs. " Damn all foreign countries," said a working-man to Mr. Gladstone in 1831; " what has Old England to do with foreign countries ? " [1] Indeed, for the moment, there seemed enough to do at home. The immediate problem was to adjust a Constitution, so often pronounced perfect in every detail, to the necessities of a new age. The middle classes of England, who now possessed a large share of the national wealth, demanded a corresponding share of political influence and, during the fourteen years which followed the Reform Bill, demonstrated the crucial fact of the Victorian Age— that England's policy was to be dictated by her shopkeepers. But to Bright and Cobden, who led the way to victory, the repeal of the Corn Laws seemed far more than a triumph of the industrial classes over the land-owners and aristocracy. They

---

[1] Morley, *Gladstone*, i. 72. " This is not the only time," remarked Mr. Gladstone, " that I have received an important lesson from a humble source."

believed that the cheering crowds who thronged
their platform spoke with the authentic voice of
the people of England. In that voice Cobden
found a certain " intuitive sagacity which had given
rise to the old adage that the voice of the people
was the voice of God." [1]   A glorious vista was
opened : the Corn Laws were but the first work of
darkness destined to be swept away by the power
of the new democracy. Wars with their accom-
panying evils of increased armaments and high
taxation would surely cease with the foundation
of an enlightened international comity. Universal
peace was the natural corollary to Free Trade.
" I believe," Cobden told an audience at Manchester in 1846, " that the desire and motive for
large and mighty empires, for gigantic armies and
great navies will die away when man becomes one
family and freely exchanges the fruits of his labour
with his brother man." [2]

In 1847, however, the Duke of Wellington,
whose past greatness and dignified old age everywhere secured for his lightest word a reverence
that was almost religious, came to the conclusion
that Louis Philippe was planning an invasion of
England. He expressed this opinion in a private
letter to a fellow officer and the letter found its way
into the public Press.[3]   To the dismay of every
newspaper reader and the astonishment of every
naval authority, the country was informed that
there was " not a spot on the coast on which
infantry might not be thrown on shore at any time
of tide, with any wind, and in any weather, and

[1] Morley, *Cobden*, i. 241.
[2] Speech, January 15, 1846.
[3] Hansard, xcvi. 909. Lord John Russell said on behalf of the
Duke that " nothing could have given greater pain [to the Duke]
than the publication of sentiments which he had expressed con-
fidentially to a brother officer."

from which such a body of infantry, so thrown on
shore, would not find within a distance of five miles
a road into the interior of the country, through
the cliffs, practicable for the march of a body of
troops." The effect of this letter was great and a
demand for an increase in our national defences
immediately followed. The Whig Ministry, which
had come into power after the fall of Sir Robert
Peel determined to bring in a Militia Bill. The
project was supported by Lord Palmerston, who
had entered upon his third term at the Foreign
Office and had once more begun that policy of
tacquinerie which so exasperated the Foreign
Ministers and Courts of Europe. Now, if ever, was
the time for Cobden and his friends to put the "intuitive sagacity" of their countrymen to the test.

Cobden did his best to transform the anti-Corn
Law League into an equally effective Peace Society.
But the task was no easy one. The League had
withstood and defeated the class of landlords,
but the new enemy was human nature itself. At
the time of the Duke's letter, Cobden wrote to John
Bright : " I have always had an instinctive mono-
mania against this system of foreign interference,
protocolling, diplomatizing, etc., and I should be
glad if you and our other free-trade friends, who
have beaten the daily broadsheets into common
sense upon another question, would oppose your-
selves to the Palmerstonian system and try to
prevent the Foreign Office from undoing the good
work which the Board of Trade has done to the
people. But you must not disguise from your-
selves that the evil has its roots in the pugnacious,
energetic, self-sufficient foreigner-despising, and
pitying character of the noble insular creature
John Bull." [1]

[1] Morley, *Cobden*, i. 507.

The newly formed Peace Society did its best to reform John Bull. During the succeeding years it held conferences in Manchester and Glasgow, in Brussels, Frankfurt, and Paris. Public meetings protested against the enterprising massacres of " Rajah Brooke " in Borneo and passed resolutions against the Kaffir War in South Africa. Such protests met with little sympathy in the Press ; and sporting papers like *Bell's Life* seemed to regard the shooting of Dyaks as a natural recreation of the Englishman when pheasants were out of season. Unfortunately, such papers as *The Illustrated London News*, with a large middle-class circulation, were equally unfavourable. " How many public men who have ambitions to gratify," Cobden wondered, " will range themselves alongside of us so long as the Press is thus opposed to them ? To change the Press we must change public opinion. And, mind, when I speak of the Press I speak of those weekly papers which are really supported by the people." [1]

Yet occasionally there was encouragement. In June 1849, Cobden had proposed in the House of Commons the adoption of the principle of arbitration. Though defeated, he procured seventy-nine votes in his favour, and *Punch*, edited by his friend, Douglas Jerrold, wrote that " the olive twig placed by Cobden in Westminster will flourish despite the blighting wit of mess rooms, and will rise and spread into a tree that shall offer shade and security for all nations." [2]

[1] Morley, *Cobden*, 2, 114. The Punjab Campaign, for instance, formed the main item of interest for several months (beginning January 27, 1849) in *The Illustrated London News*. Mackay, i. 354, estimates its circulation at this time as 60,000. For the activities of the Peace Society at this time, vide Appleton, 48–53.

[2] *Punch*, June 1849. Earlier in the same year *Punch* rebuked the Duke of Wellington for wanting to educate the army since,

Cobden's motion in favour of international arbitration represents the highest point achieved by the Peace Society for many years. A few months later an incident occurred which showed that a new spirit had appeared in English public life. A young generation of Englishmen had watched the continental revolutions of 1848 with a feeling of gratitude that England was not as other nations. European despotisms were advised to adopt a Constitution like that of England ; they, too, would find only Chartists where now they found Carbonari.[1] But in 1849 a change came. The old regime again triumphed ; the revolutionaries of 1848 were the martyrs of 1849. Englishmen read with disgust of the torture of prisoners in Lombardy and Naples, of the atrocities of Russian troops in Hungary and of the flogging of high-born ladies by General Haynau. It is probable that nothing would have come from this new liberal sympathy had the Tsar and the Austrian Emperor been content with crushing the revolution in Hungary. But they went further and demanded that Turkey should surrender those Hungarian patriots who had taken refuge in the Ottoman Empire. Encouraged by Stratford-Canning, the English ambassador at the Porte, Turkey refused. A wave of sentiment swept over England. *Punch*, hitherto so strongly non-interventionist, held up the Tsar to public execration and began to ridicule the efforts of the Peace Society.[2] Backed by this national feeling, Lord Palmerston dispatched a

if soldiers were educated, there would be no army ! Douglas Jerrold was strongly pacific in sentiment until 1849. His correspondence with Joseph Sturge on the subject is given by Richard, 406–7.

[1] Cf. *Punch*, xv. 266, where John Bull is seen showing Europe how to mix the Constitutional Plum-pudding.

[2] Ibid., xvii. cp. 63, 93, 106, 157, 167, 197.

British fleet to the Dardanelles and, whether in deference to this threat or not, the Emperors withdrew their demand.[1]

The incident left an enduring impression on the minds of thousands of Englishmen. For the first time, that middle-class public, for whose favours Cobden and Palmerston were rival suitors, became really enthusiastic on behalf of a foreign national movement. The most illustrious of the refugees, Louis Kossuth, made his way to England, and by his eloquent accounts of the horrors of 1849 prevented memory of the incident growing dim. The Tsar and the Austrian Emperor were now known to be " merciless tyrants and despots " and, by a curious accident, Turkey had taken her place among the champions of European Liberalism. Most important of all, the incident added immensely to the popularity of Lord Palmerston.

2. Lord Palmerston and the Incident of Don Pacifico.

Lord Palmerston was already over sixty years of age and had been employed in the government of England for forty years. Before the incident of the refugees he had been a popular statesman, second only to Lord John Russell among the

[1] Cobden and many others declared that the Tsar had given way before the dispatch of the fleet, but it was commonly believed that Palmerston's action had frightened the Tsar. A vigorous policy on the part of Palmerston in the preceding year might very possibly have prevented Russia from crossing the frontier to put down the Hungarian Republic. But he refused to recognize the Revolutionary Government and allowed it to be crushed without protest. European revolutionaries, therefore, liked him no better than did their enemies. Vide *The Story of Lord Palmerston*, by Karl Marx, and the speeches of Louis Kossuth. Vide also Morley, *Cobden*, ii. 34–9. A suggestive explanation of this apparent inconsistency and an account of the propaganda in English newspapers on behalf of the refugees in the autumn of 1849 is given by Sproxton, *Palmerston and the Hungarian Revolution*.

Whig leaders. But the new spirit which the reaction in Europe had roused in England gave him a greater opportunity. He knew that the policy of " non-intervention " was no longer attractive. Non-intervention in the past had meant the refusal to aid Metternich in governing Europe for the advantage of the House of Hapsburg. After 1849 non-intervention seemed national selfishness and Palmerston appealed directly to a young generation to whom the arguments of political economists, the commercial warnings of the Manchester School, and the cautious diplomacy of the old type of statesmen, seemed alike mean and cowardly. He knew that a country which had known nothing of warfare for more than thirty years was not likely to be afraid of a bold foreign policy. The actualities of the battle-field had been forgotten or had gathered round themselves that pleasant atmosphere of romantic adventure which the flags of victory, the reminiscences of veterans, and the mutual exchange of ministerial congratulations so easily substituted in time of peace. In the duel which Cobden set himself to fight with Palmerston for the capture of public opinion reasoned knowledge was on his side; but ignorance is a great asset in political controversy and the romanticism which springs from it is more than a match for self-interest, however enlightened. There was an instinctive response to Palmerston's appeal; the craving for that excitement which nineteenth-century industrialism did so little to satisfy, the pride of national greatness, the contempt for the foreigner, and the natural love of the battle which is just out of sight; all these were on Lord Palmerston's side.

He knew that blue books and diplomatic documents were tedious and, though himself necessarily concerned with them, he never made Cobden's

mistake of inflicting them on the public. He understood by instinct what Stockmar learnt by observation, that the English were not really interested
in foreign politics but in individuals.[1] While he
was in charge European diplomacy took on the
familiar appearance of a sporting arena. All was
personal and vivid. Intricate questions of policy
which Prince Albert or Lord Aberdeen found
subjects for anxious discussion and careful memoranda, were apparently regarded by Palmerston as
challenges to a boxing match ; and with delight
the public saw him rush into the fray like the warm-
hearted schoolboy of fiction who could not allow
a smaller boy to be bullied in his presence.[2] " I
have been so busy," he would say, " fighting my
battle with France that I have been obliged to put
off for a time taking up my skirmish with Russia." [3]
And when actual interference was unwise or unnecessary, he kept up the sporting metaphor and
represented himself as the cool bystander who
would keep the ring and ensure fair play. He was,
he said, the " judicious bottle-holder " and he at
once appeared in *Punch* with a straw in his mouth.

Thus his intention was always to represent
himself as the type of what Englishmen liked an
English statesman to be. Even advanced working-
men, to whom Palmerston was apt to talk like a
Manchester Liberal, found a soft place for so good
a sportsman, and David Urquhart's astonishing
energy could never convince more than a handful
that " Pam " was a traitor.[4] He cared nothing for

[1] Stockmar, ii. 347–8.

[2] So *Punch* liked to represent him. Cp. xv. " Mr. Punch's Prizes
for the Session," " Master Pam for his intrepidity in jumping
into hot water on all occasions."

[3] Ashley, i. 208.

[4] For David Urquhart, vide *Gertrude Robinson's Life.* He
organized working-men's classes for the study of foreign affairs

the opinion of foreign Courts, little for that of his fellow statesmen or even his own Foreign Office officials : statesmen might come and go but " John Bull," he believed, would go on for ever.

" As long as England is England," he declared, " as long as the English people are animated by the feelings and spirit and opinions which they possess, you may knock down twenty Foreign Ministers one after another, but depend upon it no one will keep his place who does not act upon the same principles." [1]   What these principles were he explained in his speech on the occasion of Cobden's arbitration proposal.

He was convinced, and his conviction was shared by a large number of his countrymen, that the interest of England consistently coincided with the eternal principles of morality. " I hold that the real policy of England is to be the champion of justice and right : pursuing that course with moderation and prudence, not becoming the Quixote of the world, but giving the weight of her moral sanction and support wherever she thinks justice, and whenever she thinks that wrong has been done . . . we have no eternal allies and no perpetual enemies. Our interests are eternal and perpetual, and those interests it is our duty to follow ; and if I might be allowed to express in one sentence the principle which ought to guide an English Minister, I would adopt an expression of Canning and say that with every British Minister the

at which he taught the universal danger from Russia and the sub-servience of our statesmen to the Tsar. He claimed that he had destroyed the Chartist Movement by this diversion and added : " I cannot conceive of circumstances under which I should be wrong."   For Palmerston's dealings with working-men, vide Holyoake, ii. 77, and his description of Urquhart's " Society for cutting off Palmerston's head."

[1] Ashley, i. 217.

interests of England ought to be Shibboleth of his policy." [1]

In Lord Palmerston's hands, therefore, the voter felt confident that his pride, his interest, and his conscience were all in safe keeping. He was in a peculiar manner a representative man : in Lord John Russell's phrase he was a " Minister of England." For the most part he assumed this character by instinct. But there was something further that has not been understood by his biographers. He was quite conscious that he relied on forces in the national system which other Foreign Ministers were wont to neglect. He belonged to a political party, but it was his object to transcend party issues. His appeal was, in the strict sense of the word, a democratic one. He never missed an opportunity of appearing to advantage in a daily paper. Every political group employed some newspaper to represent its point of view, and even, on occasion, to make official statements on its behalf, but Palmerston was probably the first English statesman who deliberately ingratiated himself with papers of all shades of opinion. After his death, the editor of a prominent paper wrote : " There was never a man who was so great a favourite personally, not with the reporters only, but with all the gentlemen filling the higher positions on the Press, as the late Lord Palmerston. The reporters of all the papers, without reference to the point as to whether the paper they represented were favourable or opposed to his Government, vied with each other in their anxiety to pay attention to whatever he said." Neither was their favour wholly unsolicited. " It often happened during the prolonged Premiership or Foreign Secretaryship of Lord Palmerston, that on representing

[1] Ashley, i. 62–3.

to him both in Hants or at Tiverton that if the time fixed for his speech could not be altered, the reporters from London would not be able to reach their respective offices with their report until too late, he would immediately apply to alter the programmes so that the reporters should not be disappointed." And, on occasions when an alteration of the programme would not serve, he was willing to make private orations in his room at the hotel, which the reporters could convey punctually, for the morning's paper.[1]

It was this personal appeal to the public which differentiated Lord Palmerston from other statesmen of his period and which so often infuriated them. He knew that if he was sufficiently popular he could do what he liked. "Palmerston," wrote Bulwer Lytton, "is Mamma England's spoilt child, and the more mischief he does the more she admires him. What a spirit he has! cries Mamma, and smash goes the crockery!" And he was just as cheerful, jaunty, some called it, whether it was the national or the party crockery that went smash. His actions as Foreign Minister were his own, not those of his Government and, when he spoke in Parliament, he was not so much concerned with the faces he saw round him as with the greater public which would read his speech in the newspaper the next morning.[2] Thus he cared little to answer particular objections raised against him : he was interested in enunciating some general principle which would make his speech memorable all over the country, or in taunting his opponents in a manner which would amuse even where it did not

[1] Grant, ii. 205–8; Robinson, 224–5; Grev., iv. 123.
[2] He appears to have been one of the few English statesmen whose words were always audible in the Reporter's Gallery. Cp. Grant, 201 ff.

convince. Arguments of policy he met with arguments *ad hominem*.   When he could not answer
Cobden's unexpected facts he felt no embarrassment
as Peel did under similar circumstances : he repelled the facts with gibes.   He always assumed,
for instance, that a Manchester non-interventionist
was an extreme pacifist who was ready to sell his
country for money.   On one occasion John Bright
described his method : In answer to a remark to
this effect, " I wonder if the country were invaded
what the Peace Society would do ? "   John Bright
replied that Lord Palmerston used to say they
(the Peace Society) would go with their hands full
of money and say to the invader : " How much will
you take to go away ? "   " But," Mr. Bright
concluded, " I never doubted that when there was
a nation that accepted the laws of Christ, and sought
to act them out, and sought to live consistently
among these other nations, and carried out the
influence of the Christian spirit in its relation with
others, I never doubted in my life that the Eternal
would take care of that nation." [1]

Cobden, who was not granted his friend's intimate
knowledge of the ways of Providence, found it less
easy to reply.   He was conscious of the sufferings
of oppressed nations and was anxious, in extreme
cases, to organize public opinion in their favour.
When he admitted this, Palmerston asked a further
question : Had public opinion any value unless
supported by guns and soldiers in the background ?
Cobden had been willing to speak at a meeting to
welcome Kossuth : what would he have done if
Russia had pressed her claims a little further in
1849 ? Would Cobden have withdrawn and left
him to the mercies of Radetzky or Haynau, or
would he, too, have forgotten the policy of non-

[1] Speech at Llandudno, 23/11/76.

intervention and believed with Palmerston that the time had come for gunboats ? [1]

Palmerston's speeches were not all banter or all argument. He mingled elements acceptable to every section of his audience, and so great was his skill that all but the few who carefully studied his argument found themselves in agreement. He knew nothing of the technique he was employing, but he was probably one of the greatest masters in the art of speaking in elusive general terms, calculated to rouse enthusiasm among his supporters without appearing dangerous to any but his most violent opponents. These latter served his purpose as objects of ridicule.

Lord Palmerston, then, relied on the fact that " Mamma England " was fond of him. Between 1846 and 1850 he put her affection to the test by breaking an almost excessive amount of crockery. During these four years he quarrelled with the French, Austrian, Russian, and Spanish Governments, and had come near, as it seemed, to fighting all of them in turn ; sometimes he was meddling in Switzerland, sometimes wrangling with Louis Philippe and Guizot concerning the Spanish marriages ; now he was encouraging Italian patriots and now suggesting a constitution to the Pope ; again he was aiding the revolution in Portugal or coercing the Tsar in aid of Hungarian refugees in Turkey. But at last, in the summer of 1850, many thought that he had passed even the latitude allowed to the favourite child. England was isolated in Europe. It seemed that a European war was just about to break out because Lord Palmerston supported the claims of a certain Don Pacifico, who had failed to receive compensation from the Government of Greece for

[1] Hobson, 74–9.

property which had been injured by an Athenian mob.

The prosecution of these claims had led to imminent danger of war with France and at that moment British gunboats were bombarding a Greek port and challenging Russia to join with France against us. Many thought this an expensive way of collecting the doubtful debts of a disreputable Portuguese Jew, even though he happened to be a British subject. Palmerston's enemies saw their chance. France and Russia had reached the end of their patience ; Lord John had nearly reached the end of his. The Russian Minister was threatening to follow M. Drouyn de Lluys who had already quitted London. It seemed likely that Lord John, finding England's good faith was imperilled as well as war threatened, would prefer to dismiss Palmerston without himself resigning. " At last," wrote Greville, " there seems a tolerable chance of Palmerston coming to grief." The Cabinet, however, resolved " to do nothing " and to hope that the " rickety concern will scramble on as heretofore." [1]

The Opposition, therefore, brought a concerted attack upon the Government's foreign policy. Lord Derby moved a vote of censure in the House of Lords and carried it by a substantial majority. In the House of Commons debate which followed, every political group pronounced with unusual clearness its opinion not merely of the Don Pacifico incident but on the whole question of an English statesman's duty in foreign affairs.

It was not till the second night that Palmerston spoke. He knew that there were four main sections of opinion in the House. Since Lord John Russell had resolved to support him he was sure of the

[1] Grev., vi. 332–42.

Whig vote, but there were many who, though giving his policy general support, thought that on this occasion he had exposed the country to unnecessary risks.[1]   He hoped, if possible, to transform these party voters into firm adherents of his own.

In the second place there was the Manchester School whose underlying disunity was not yet apparent.   For the time it was strongly pacific and composed of business men who believed in Free Trade and peace as a path to prosperity, and of more extreme pacifists, many of whom were Quakers.   But for the moment they were all strong "non-interventionists" and opposed to Palmerston's whole view of foreign policy.

Thirdly, he had to meet the old school of Conservative non-interventionists.   Sir Robert Peel in his last speech voiced its views and Mr. Gladstone supported him with telling eloquence.[2]   Peel showed that his position was that which Canning had adopted at the Congress of Verona.   It was not our business to interfere by aiding the revolutionaries of Europe any more than it was right for us to aid Metternich in upholding despotisms like that of King Bomba.   His principle was easily definable, "namely, non-interference with the domestic affairs of other countries without some clear and undeniable necessity arising from the

[1] Cp. *Spectator*, 29/6/50.

[2] This speech is particularly notable because Mr. Gladstone did not frequently indulge in humour.   After describing the extravagance of Don Pacifico's claims he continued, "So, Sir, having his house crammed full of fine furniture, fine clothes, and fine jewels, Mr. Pacifico was in all other respects a pauper."   This furniture all so "massive and solid was utterly destroyed," and yet there was no fire.   "Why, Sir, they could not without fire thus have destroyed such articles unless, indeed, they had eaten them." Hansard, cxii. 563.

circumstances, affecting the interests of your own
country." [1]

Lastly, the Derbyites attacked Lord Palmerston
not so much because he interfered abroad as because
they considered that he habitually did so on the
wrong side. In this case they led the attack
against him because they saw in the Greek dispute
an opportunity for weakening and perhaps destroying the Whig Government, on the grounds
that our claims in the East were entirely inde-
fensible and had left England without a friend
in Europe.

Confronted with this combined attack, Lord
Palmerston set himself not only to answer his
opponents, but also, if possible, to win them.
The Manchester School he left alone. Flippancy,
his usual method of dealing with Cobden and his
friends, was out of place on this occasion and, in
any case, he had no hope of winning their votes.

His object was to convince the Tories and the
Whigs that in the general question of the conduct of
foreign affairs they were in substantial agreement.
He hoped to show that his policy was not Whig or
Tory, but " English."

He therefore began by accusing his opponents
of making a party issue of a matter which, he said,
demanded more than a mere expression of opinion
in the House of Lords. He stated that the resolution which had been accepted there laid down
that " British subjects in foreign lands are entitled
to nothing but the protection of the laws and the
tribunals of the land in which they happen to
reside." [2] He thus took the debate as far as

[1] Sir Robert Peel was thrown from his horse on the day of his
speech and died two days later. His death removed the most
powerful of Lord Palmerston's political opponents.

[2] The actual words of the resolution in the Lords were : " To
resolve that while the House fully recognizes the right and duty

possible from the narrow question of our policy
in Greece by interpreting the resolution in a way
which only Mr. Gladstone and a few of his most
critical opponents realized that it could not bear.
He proceeded to show that it outlined a position
which no Foreign Minister would find tolerable.
That recourse should first be had to the Courts of
the foreign country he willingly admitted, but
what was to be done in countries where legality
was a fraud and justice a synonym for cruelty and
extortion ? Drawing pictures of Englishmen robbed,
tortured, bastinadoed, executed on false witness,
he asked his non-interventionist critics, his dubious
friends and Tory libellers whether any Foreign
Minister could avoid interference in such cases ?
Cheers assured him that he could not. In the
atmosphere thus created it was easy to refute
actual charges without referring in too much detail
to the difficult points connected with Don Pacifico's
claim of £50 for a "lit conjugal " and £170 for a
drawing-room sofa.

Having thus taken the war into the enemies'
camp, he proceeded to rout them by a veiled but
quite easily discernible accusation that the reason
for this attack on the Government was a foreign
intrigue. He was being attacked because Russian
and French Ministers hated him.[1] It was these
supporters of Court parties and reactionary Ministers who were the real revolutionaries ; " the blind-

of the Government to secure to Her Majesty's subjects residing
in Foreign States the full protection of the Laws of these States,
it regrets to find, by the Correspondence recently laid upon the
Table by Her Majesty's Command, that various claims against
the Greek Government, doubtful in point of justice, or exaggerated
in amount have been enforced by coercive measures directed against
the Commerce and People of Greece, and calculated to endanger
the continuance of our Friendly relations with other Powers."

[1] Vide Ashley, i. 218-19.

minded men who dam up the current of human
improvement until the irresistible pressure of accu-
mulated discontent breaks down those very institutions which a timely application of renovating
means would have rendered strong and lasting."

Palmerston so far had answered the charges against
him, and discredited his opponents by the simple
process of assuming that they held a doctrine and
adopted a method of attack which had been far
from their thoughts. It was now time to justify
himself before that larger tribunal whose existence
he never forgot. Don Pacifico, he knew, mattered
little to anyone, and would soon be forgotten. But
the principles by which he defended his conduct of
foreign affairs only needed embodiment in a striking
phrase to appeal to every hearer and newspaper
reader. There is, as Gladstone pointed out next
day, no real analogy between the English subject,
travelling in countries which possess their own
laws and civilization, and the Roman citizen of
the Empire, dwelling among conquered and semi-
barbaric peoples whose only law and justice came
from their conquerors. But there were few Englishmen who did not respond to Palmerston's appeal,
when leaving the politics of party and the immediate
matter under discussion, he cried that a British
subject should be able to say: " Civis Romanus
sum " and, in whatever land he might be, feel:
" Confident that the watchful eye and the strong
arm of England will protect him against injustice
and wrong."

His speech, with its wonderful peroration, drew
applause from his bitterest opponents. Greville,
to whom Palmerston represented everything undesirable, did not hear the speech, but read it in the
calm of his study. He noted in his diary that
Palmerston " came out with prodigious force and

success. . . . It was impossible to deny its great ability : parts of it are strikingly eloquent and inimitably adroit. The ability of it is the more remarkable because on an attentive and calm perusal of it, the insufficiency of it as an answer and defence against the various charges which have been brought against him is manifest."

This, no doubt, was true, but Greville missed the real significance of the debate when he added that Palmerston had done no more than " adorn his speech with a profusion of magnificent and successful claptraps." [1] He had done far more : he had fixed in the minds of Englishmen a permanent picture of true English behaviour. The phrase " Civis Romanus sum " might be forgotten, but the idea to which he gave form has never since left English politics. Since 1850, every English Foreign Minister has been compelled to conform, in some degree, to this pattern.

The immediate considerations were equally significant. It was Lord Palmerston who had gained in popularity, not the Whig Government. " These discussions and attacks," wrote Greville, " which were to have shaken him in his seat, have only made him more powerful than he was before, but whether they have strengthened the Government is another question." Another question ! Apparently Palmerston thought it an irrelevant one. He seemed less and less to concern himself with his colleagues and during the next eighteen months at the Foreign Office he behaved as if he alone was responsible for England's honour. Unknown to the public he was now engaged in a furious struggle with Prince Albert and the Queen, and Lord John's position between a recalcitrant

[1] Grev., vi. 353-4.

Foreign Minister and an angry Crown became increasingly difficult.[1]

One further incident occurred in 1850 which, by weakening the position of Lord John and reinforcing the idea that foreign potentates were all enemies of England, indirectly favoured the position of Lord Palmerston. The incident of the " Papal Aggression " is perhaps as curious as any in the history of nineteenth-century public opinion. A papal Bull announced that Roman bishoprics were to be established in England. A wave of angry Protestantism swept over England. The ancient tradition of hatred and fear of the Papacy had never died. The feeling which had hunted priests in the sixteenth century, made civil war and revolution in the seventeenth century, persecution and Gordon Riots in the eighteenth, revived as implacable as ever. Newspapers, letters, pamphlets, cartoons, public meetings, popular songs all continued to pour forth anger and execration on the heads of the Pope, Dr. Wiseman, and his colleagues.[2] A

[1] Strachey, chap. v.

[2] *Punch*, vol. 19. All the political cartoons and many articles for almost six months deal with the " Papal Aggression." Cp. also a popular ballad preserved in the British Museum :

"CARDINAL WISEMAN.

" Good people, pray listen, I'll tell you a joke
That was tried on us English by the foolish Pope,
Who sent us a *Bull*, Oh ! What an old bloak !
To try such a thing in old England.
In Old England 'twill never go down !

"Oh ! Cardinal Wiseman you must be a flat,
To try in Old England to wear the red hat,
Who would think a *Wiseman* so foolish as that !
To wear such a thing in Old England.
In Old England 'twill never go down.

"Little Lord John he penn'd a sharp note
To the Bishop of Durham concerning the Pope,
And another fat churchman who was turning his coat,
But if he does he'll be turned from Old England.
In England 'twill never go down ! "

5

backwash of the torrent struck the Puseyites and, though the agitation spent itself after the introduction of an Ecclesiastical Titles Bill, those who dared to vote against its inoperative provisions were always liable to the charge of being Papists. Lord John Russell shared the popular excitement, and in an open letter to the Bishop of Durham identified himself with the most extreme of the Protestants. Though he gained a temporary increase of popularity in the country, he roused a bitter antagonism among the Irish members, and alienated many moderate men who might have been willing to accept his leadership in the future.[1] But the picture that Lord Palmerston had drawn was but lined in more deeply. The Pope had taken his place side by side with the other tyrants and enemies of liberty—Bomba, the Austrian Emperor, and the Tsar. "The Pope," declared one newspaper editor, "means that Wiseman shall rule the foreign policy of England instead of Lord Palmerston."[2]

3. The Dismissal of Lord Palmerston and the French Panic.

On May 1, 1851, the Great Exhibition was opened to the public. The erection of this immense pile of glass containing examples of industrial

[1] Russell, 256. "My purpose was fully answered. Those who wished to give the Pope the right of appointing bishops in England opposed the Bill. When my object had been gained I had no objection to the repeal of the Act." It is curious to notice that one of these who suffered most for his opposition to the Ecclesiastical Titles Bill was Mr. Gladstone, afterwards so redoubtable an opponent of Papal pretensions. Vide a letter from the Hon. Emily Eden to Clarendon. (Maxwell, i. 352–3.) "As for Mr. Gladstone I rather expected that if he came into power, we might any of us be burnt at Smithfield on his warrant and under the eyes of Cardinals Philpotts and Wilberforce."

[2] Glenesk, 58.

enterprise from all parts of the world, seemed to many who visited it more than a mere work of art : it stood as a symbol of the victory of international brotherhood and mutual dependence. A strenuous attack had been made on the project by "a set of fashionables and protectionists," [1] but the Prince Consort and his Committee had routed them. Even the persistent outcry against the desecration of Hyde Park [2] had been quieted. Some observers felt that the very arrangements and organization were symbolic of those principles which were expressed so eloquently in the speeches : coercion was to disappear and commercial pacifism win its tardy battle. " It was a wonderful spectacle to see the countless multitudes streaming along in every direction and congregated upon each bank of the Serpentine; hardly any policemen to be seen and yet all so orderly and good-humoured." [3] Yet the policeman still remained a necessary feature of English society, and it is doubtful if the moral lesson of the Exhibition had penetrated as deeply as its more enthusiastic supporters believed.[4] At any rate the British public was not disposed to a mere promiscuous benevolence. In the autumn

[1] *Letters*, ii. 383.

[2] Martin, ii. 285–6, 290–1.

[3] Grev., vi. 413.

[4] A contemporary broadside, now preserved in the British Museum, suggests that a national rather than an international interpretation could be placed upon the Exhibition :—

> " THE CRYSTAL PALACE.
> " From every quarter of the Globe
> They come across the sea,
> Right to the Crystal Palace
> The wonder for to see.
> Raised by the handiwork of men
> Born on British ground,
> A challenge to the universe
> Its equal to be found."

of the same year, Louis Kossuth reached England
and was everywhere received by the populace with
almost regal honours. At Douglas Jerrold's suggestion a collection of pence was made to be spent
on a presentation copy of Shakespeare in com-
memoration of the fact that, while in an Austrian
prison, Kossuth had first studied the English
language in the works of the English national poet.
Nearly ten thousand pennies were collected, and at
a meeting at the London Tavern, presided over by
Dudley Stuart, M.P., a gorgeously bound edition
of Knight's Shakespeare, ornamented with the arms
of the Kossuth family, decorated in crimson silk
and gold, and enclosed in a wrought case, was
presented to the Hungarian hero amidst intense
enthusiasm.[1] Lord Palmerston, who had only with
difficulty been prevented from receiving Kossuth
in his own house, made no effort to hide his sympathy, and when the inhabitants of Finsbury and
Islington presented him with an address describing
the Emperors of Austria and Russia as " odious
and detestable assassins," he allowed it to be seen
that his hearty endorsement of their phraseology
was only prevented by his position as Foreign
Secretary.

Three months later an event occurred which
seemed for the moment to be the end of Lord
Palmerston. The struggle between the Crown and
the Foreign Minister, which had been raging in
secret from the early days of the Government, now
came to a head. At the beginning of December
Louis Napoleon carried out a successful *coup
d'état* in Paris. In spite of definite instructions
not to depart from a policy of neutrality Lord
Palmerston signified to the French ambassador
his complete approval of Napoleon's action,

[1] Robinson, 337–9.

and Lord John, exasperated beyond measure, at length satisfied the Court by dismissing him. The opportunity seemed an excellent one, " for this time he had been at once both indiscreet and undemocratic." [1]

Indeed, his action is not easy to explain. We know now that he did everything in his power to cultivate good relations with Louis Napoleon, and that his connection with Walewski was one of unusual intimacy and his private sources of information from France extensive. Possibly he was exceptionally long-sighted and realized that we should eventually need the friendship of Napoleon against Russia. [2] More probably he simply approved of Louis Napoleon because his triumph meant the discomforture of the Guizot party and made hopeless the cause of Orleans as well as that of the Socialists. But whatever his reasons, he seemed to be permanently prevented from plaguing further the Cabinets of Europe.

In the debate which followed his dismissal, Lord John seemed to triumph overwhelmingly. He read to the astonished House a memorandum which had been sent to Lord Palmerston by the Queen in the preceding year. It stated with unusual frankness that the Queen would be justified in dismissing a Foreign Minister who " arbitrarily altered or modified " documents to which the Royal sanction had been given and, in effect, reminded Lord Palmerston that the Foreign Secretary was responsible to the Crown. [3] Greville made a note in his diary of the impression produced in the House. " In all my experience I never recollect such a triumph as John Russell achieved or such

---

[1] Simpson, 165.
[2] This was Stockmar's view. *Memoirs*, ii. 463.
[3] *Letters*, ii. 238, 264.

a complete discomforture as Palmerston's. Lord John made a very able speech, and disclosed as much as was necessary and no more. Beyond all doubt his great *coup* was the Queen's Minute of 1850, which was absolutely crushing. Some grave persons think the introduction of her name was going too far, but it was irresistible. The effect was prodigious. Palmerston was weak and inefficient, and it is pretty certain was unprepared for all that Lord John brought forward." [1]

Even Palmerston's best friends thought his position almost hopeless, while Disraeli expressed the usual view when he said: "There *was* a Palmerston." [2] As a matter of fact, it is unlikely that any incident of his career proved, in the long run, so greatly to his advantage. Crushed for the moment in the House, he resorted to a weapon he had already used in 1850. He declared himself a victim of foreign intrigue. From this time onward he made this plea the strength of his position. His colleagues, perhaps, were subservient to foreign influence, to Guizot or perhaps to German or Russian Courts : he alone, who had stood foursquare against the enemies of England, had paid the penalty. [3] Macaulay, sitting next Thiers at breakfast a few weeks later, remarked of Palmerston : "Après avoir été l'apôtre des idées libérales, il a été le martyr du pouvoir arbitraire." "Mon Dieu !" said Thiers, "et c'est un Anglais qui a dit ça."

[1] Grev., vi. 455. Cp. Simpson, 166, for the interesting new point that Normanby himself had expressed a long-winded approval of the *coup d'état* which Palmerston might have used in his defence had he troubled to read his ambassador's reports in full.

[2] Cf. Dalling's letter, Ashley, i. 330–1.

[3] Ashley, i. 225 ; Martin, ii. 280 ; Granville, i. 45 ; Hayward, i. 164. The Duke of Newcastle wrote : "I fancy some intrigue in France must be the real cause."

The most curious feature of the situation was that the occasion of Palmerston's dismissal was his approval of the destruction of French Liberalism. A few English Liberals were puzzled at the defection of their leader. The *Westminster* noted the fact and frankly gave it up: " We are inclined to think that even in that act of treason towards liberty his Lordship was not unactuated by a liberal, however mistaken and mysterious a motive." [1]

But, for the most part, Palmerston's supporters in the country refused to believe that he could have approved of the behaviour of Napoleon whom they regarded as the new menace to European freedom. It seemed that Palmerston had reached an eminence which shut out the view of such ironical facts. " Every event in which Palmerston is concerned ends in his standing higher than he did before," said one observer.[2] The Tories were divided : some hoped that the Whig Government could not stand without him, while *The Times* supported the Government.[3] *Reynolds's* told its Socialist readers that " though certainly no admirers of Lord Palmerston's foreign policy, we cannot but consider his dismissal . . . an unworthy concession to the Court at Vienna " and explained that the real cause of his dismissal was the incident of the Kossuth address. Ministerial explanations, which had seemed so effective in Parliament, dissolved in the heat of national popularity. The occasion of his dismissal was at once forgotten, but the fact that he had been dismissed at the wish of the Court was remembered

[1] Westminster, vol. lvii. 592.
[2] Reid, i. 490.
[3] *M.H.*, 4/2/52. " Palmerston had the best of the argument." Before the meeting of Parliament the *M.H.* declared that it did not believe one word of " the pretence that his dismissal was due to his foreign policy." Cp. *Times*, 25/12/51.

and was to have unexpected results.[1] In fact, the

[1] The following popular song illustrates the way in which Lord Palmerston's dismissal was regarded outside Parliamentary circles.

"ENGLAND AND NAPOLEON.

I

" Oh ! Have you heard the news of late,
    The Whigs are in a cranky state,
    And they'll find out when its too late,
        They're done for by their snarling ;
    For small Lord John has been and gone
    And turned adrift Lord Palmerston,
    Amongst the lot the only don,
    Who didn't take care of number one ;
    Out spoke Home Secretary Gray,
    I wish old Palmy was away,
    Aye, turn him out they all did say,
        For he's the people's darling.

II

" In every foreign Court his name,
    Upheld Old England's glorious fame,
    And all our enemies were tame
        Because he kept them under.
    But now in Austria's tyrant Court,
    They did chuckle all in glee and sport,
    Because they've heard the glad report
    Says young Napoleon ' that's your sort ' ;
    But let them laugh who win the day,
    He'll live to make them dearly pay,
    That aught against him they did say ;
        And if he don't I'll wonder.

III

" Whene'er doth meet the Parliament,
    The Whigs to pot will straight be sent,
    That humbug of a Government
        Won't live a moment longer.
    Then Palmy he'll be at our head,
    And keep the tyrants all in dread,
    Austria and France will wish him dead
    And for a milksop in his stead,
    Haynau and the Russian Tsar,
    Will curse him in their realms afar.
    And on their feelings it will jar,
        To find old Palmy stronger.

" grave persons " of whom Greville spoke, had been
more farsighted than usual : Lord John would have
done well to withold the Queen's Memorandum, to
resist the irresistible. The blow would have been

IV

" Young Nap would like his father be,
He hates the manly and the free,
And now an army large has he,
    Upon our shores to thunder.
The Frenchmen with their fierce moustachious,
Are now to settle all our hashes,
And Haynau with a whip to lash us
Will feel too glad if he can thrash us.
From Fleet Street along the Strand,
French Cuirasiers will have command,
The Marseillaise will play each band,
    The Life Guards will knock under.

V

" Young Nap upon a prancing horse,
Will yell out French until he's hoarse,
Come, shoot them down my gallant force
    And make your sabres gory.
You well remember Waterloo,
Where these vile English overthrew
Our soldiers and my uncle to[o].
Amongst our ranks their bullets flew,
You now can pay them what they gave,
Make every Englishman a slave,
No more they're rulers of the wave,
    And sunk is England's glory.

VI

" Old Wellington, that queer old chap,
At Apsley House now takes a nap,
I'll catch him straightway in a trap
    And take him over the water.
But what is that which now he hears,
A glorious burst of British cheers,
Were done for bayonets and spears,
The British Army swiftly nears
A thundering charge our Life Guards make,
The would-be Emperor they take,
The Frenchmen's ranks like chaff they break
    And make them run with slaughter."

less crushing it is true, but one could have been surer of the rebound.

Lord Palmerston thoroughly enjoyed his position. He stood, as he loved to do, between and above parties. Lord John still accepted Lady Palmerston's invitations and the Derby party made constant bids for his alliance. He judged it best to wait and remain, as it were, a party by himself. Everyone was complimentary to him now, he said, since no one knew which way the cat would jump.[1]

The occasion to demonstrate his power soon came. Certainly logic had little to do either with his policy or his popularity. Though dismissed on account of his friendliness for Louis Napoleon he nevertheless shared in the belief that an invasion of England by the Emperor of France was probable. Early in the session of 1852 Lord John, in deference to the French panic which had now revived with far more than its previous intensity, brought in a Bill for organizing a militia on a local basis. Palmerston at once argued that the measure was insufficient and defeated it by a destructive amendment which insisted on the new militia being regular and national. Lord John was forced to resign, while the House, as Lord Palmerston noted with some complacency, cheered him " in a most insulting manner." " I have had my tit for tat with John Russell," he wrote to his brother immediately afterwards.[2] There could be no doubt now that he and not Lord John was the most popular Minister in the country.

On the fall of the Whig Ministry Lord Derby, after great difficulty, succeeded in forming a Government. Having failed to secure the adherence of Palmerston, and being still committed to a Protectionist policy the new administration never

[1] Grev., vi. 456–7; Dasent, 151; Glenesk, 72.   [2] Ashley, i. 334.

appeared likely to be of long duration. The country was in a state of violent agitation. A Napoleon was once more Emperor in France. Who could doubt that he would attempt to avenge his uncle ? In these days of steamships he " could easily land fifty or sixty thousand troops on the south coast in a single night."

A French fleet was being built secretly at Cherbourg, another was discovered in the Seine. Was it possible, some asked, that England had really fallen on days of decadence and was afraid of the French ? Had England indeed become a nation of shopkeepers ? Some believed that the fear of France, whether justified by facts or not, had a beneficial effect on the national character : it roused once again the heroic spirit in the rising generation, many of whom no doubt itched, after the manner of Nevil Beauchamp, to pen a personal challenge to the presumptuous officers of France. The newspapers did their best to encourage this spirit. One of the most influential journalists wrote : " Nor is it in my opinion useless or un-necessary to keep alive in England a strong feeling on this subject. This nation is a good deal ener-vated by a long peace, by easy habits of inter-course, by peace societies, and false economy. . . . Happen what may, there is nothing so important as to sustain a tone of moral independence and a clear judgment among the people of England, who will grudge no sacrifices if they are convinced that the principles they cherish are even indirectly threatened from abroad." [1]

[1] Reeve, i. 251. For the " Panic," vide periodical literature of 1852, e.g. *Blackwood's*, July ; " Letters from an Englishman " in *The Times*, beginning December 20, 1851 ; Cobden's " Three Panics " ; *The Perils of Portsmouth*, by James Fergusson, Esq., and others by Sir Francis Head and Sir Charles Napier ; vide also Hansard, cxix., debates on the Militia Bill ; Meredith, chap. i.

In November the Duke of Wellington died.   His funeral was a military pageant which emphasized the majesty of British arms and reminded thousands of onlookers that Napoleon would have conquered had not England been greatly led.   Verses poured from the Press expressing the national grief and the fear that England was no longer ready to meet the foe.   Tennyson, in a less transitory poem, voiced the sentiment of the moment when he said that "The last great Englishman is low."

> A people's voice! We are a people yet.
> Tho' all men else their nobler dreams forget,
> Confused by brainless mobs and lawless Powers;
> Thank Him who isled us here, and roughly set
> His Briton in blown seas and storming showers,
> We have a voice, with which to pay the debt
> Of boundless love and reverence and regret
> To those great men who fought, and kept it ours.
> And keep it ours, O God, from brute control;
> O Statesmen, guard us, guard the eye, the soul
> Of Europe, keep our noble England whole,
> And save the one true seed of freedom sown
> Betwixt a people and their ancient throne,
> That sober freedom out of which there springs
> Our loyal passion for our temperate kings;
> For, saving that, ye help to save mankind
> Till public wrong be crumbled into dust,
> And drill the raw world for the march of mind,
> Till crowds at length be sane and crowns be just.
> But wink no more in slothful overtrust.
> Remember him who led your hosts;
> He bade you guard the sacred coasts.[1]

What statesman was there whom the people could trust to guard their sacred coast? Was England, bereft of the Duke, an open prey to the despoiler? Who now would guard her virgin honour? The task, by an almost universal consent, devolved upon Lord Palmerston.

[1] "Ode on the Death of the Duke of Wellington," 1852.

CHAPTER IV

THE ABERDEEN CABINET AND THE NEWSPAPERS

(1853)

1. The Aberdeen Cabinet.

In December fell the short-lived Derby Ministry. Disraeli's Budget was thrown out by the combined vote of Whigs, Peelites, and Radicals. Since the split in the Tory Party, caused by Sir Robert Peel's conversion to Free Trade in 1846, no political group had found itself strong enough to form a stable Ministry. A Coalition was now inevitable. The difficulty was to find an acceptable Premier. Lord John Russell had lost his prestige as leader of the Whigs. His imprudence during the " Papal aggression " incident had alienated the Irish vote and made it impossible for the Peelites to work under him. Moreover, Palmerston, though willing to act in the same Ministry with Lord John, was determined never again to serve in a Cabinet with Lord John as Premier. The idea that Lord John might some day serve under Palmerston's leadership had not yet occurred to anyone.

The Tories were scarcely in a better case. The Derbyites had followers, but few leaders and no policy ; the Peelites were a party of leaders without followers. Neither could form a Government alone. There were, therefore, two possibilities. The Peelites were willing to serve under Lord

perhaps the most genuinely disinterested Prime Minister England has ever had.

These qualities carried with them certain disadvantages. He had almost fifty years of political experience, but he had not become a politician.[1] He was always something of a recluse. His reserve, chilling at first, was the result of a quite unaffected shyness. He was singularly trustful,[2] highly sensitive, and in these conflicts which commonly bring politicians the joy of warfare, he found only pain and a sense of failure. Thus he was sometimes lacking in strength if only because he preferred to give way rather than to press a point at the cost of rancour. But, like many shy men, when stung by opposition and forced to do battle for his principles he was apt to do so with an ill grace. On such occasions he was tactless and sarcastic. He lacked geniality and lightness of touch, and easily displayed a contempt for his opponents if they adopted what seemed to him a vulgar attitude. Thus there was a certain basis of truth beneath the words of his bitterest and least fair critic. Mr. Disraeli wrote of him : " His manner, arrogant and yet timid ; his words insolent and yet obscure ; his sneer, icy as Siberia ; his sarcasms drear and barren as the steppes." [3]

Yet the failure of the Aberdeen Government cannot be attributed to the defective leadership of its Premier. For some months, indeed, the Cabinet was uniformly successful, and but for the Eastern Question this success would probably have continued. In the face of this problem the ordinary

[1] He had first entered politics as early as 1803, and had been concerned in forming Pitt's last Coalition.

[2] Morley, *Gladstone*, Appendix.

[3] The Press, 4/6/53. Cp. Grev., viii. 71. Also Mr. Gladstone's letter to Arthur Gordon, *Edinburgh*, vol. 158, 375.

conventions of Cabinet procedure proved insufficient to produce the high degree of corporate activity which became suddenly necessary. It brought out the keenest of political partisanship; it tempted those who knew nothing of the Near East to hide their ignorance in the hope that others knew little more. Successful co-operation could only have been attained by complete frankness and the submission of individual prejudice to expert knowledge.[1] The traditions of Cabinet Government would have suggested the former, but never the latter. It therefore happened that none of the important initial questions were ever decided. Aberdeen, Clarendon, Lord John, and Palmerston all acted as their own experts. They never reached any agreement as to the strength of Turkey or the intentions of the Tsar.[2] Nor did they admit openly their fears as to Napoleon's honesty or Lord Stratford's intrigues. They never faced such fundamental questions as, for instance, whether it would be possible to defeat the Tsar without the aid of Austria.[3] They even let their own political necessities prejudge matters of fact, which only a special training and a first-hand knowledge could decide. Perhaps Lord Aberdeen's letter to Sir James Graham on September 6, 1853, is as good an example of the misuse of the expert adviser as could anywhere be found.

[1] Cp. Graham Wallas, "Our Social Heritage," 69–72.
[2] *Cam. Hist.*, ii. 375.
[3] It is interesting to note that Prince Albert and the Queen realized the need for being sure of such a point before declaring war. *Letters*, iii. 14–17.
Prince Albert wrote on January 24, 1854, that the worst thing about the war is that " it cannot be carried on to any effective end. Russia is a vast and ponderous mass upon which blows in the few spots where they can be planted will make no impression. If Prussia and Austria go with us, then the case is altered and war becomes practically impossible for Russia." *Correspondence.*

" We [the Cabinet]," he wrote, " decided that we might postpone any consideration respecting the removal of the fleet from Besika Bay, in consequence of our persuasion that it might remain in safety for some time longer : certainly for the whole of this month. It would be desirable, however, that we should have some naval authority to sanction this decision, and I should be obliged to you if you would have the goodness to *procure some statement to this effect.*"[1]

Even the weather was subject to the commands of the Aberdeen Government. It was politically desirable that the fleet should remain in Besika Bay through September : it followed that the autumnal storms should not this year commence until October.

But criticism of this sort is of the twentieth century. Contemporary observers felt no forebodings. In January 1853 the new Government seemed likely to pursue a harmonious course in foreign politics. " England," wrote Lord Aberdeen to the King of the Belgians, " will occupy her true position in Europe as the constant advocate of moderation and peace."[2] Who would prevent it ? Palmerston, it is true, differed fundamentally from Aberdeen on foreign affairs, and on this ground had at first hesitated to join the Cabinet.[3] But he was safely at the Home Office and not directly responsible for our foreign policy. Nor was he ever a lover of war ; he was merely willing to risk more than other people. The only European complication at the moment was the popular agitation against Napoleon III, and Lord Palmerston, so far from leading in this

---

[1] *Correspondence*, 6/9/53.   (My italics.)
[2] Morley, *Gladstone*, i. 449.
[3] Ibid., 477.   Ashley, ii. 1.

hostility, was more inclined to be friendly to France than any of his colleagues.

For the rest, the Cabinet was strongly pacific. No member of the Manchester School could have hated war with more sincerity than the Premier. Alone among the statesmen of the period, he had seen a living battle-field. After witnessing Leipsic, in the company of Prince Metternich, he had written : " It must be owned that a victory is a fine thing, but one should be at a distance to appreciate it."[1]

Lord Aberdeen's detestation of a " sporting " foreign policy was shared by the large majority of his colleagues. Mr. Gladstone, Sidney Herbert, Sir James Graham, and the Duke of Newcastle had all voted against Lord Palmerston in the affair of Don Pacifico, and Mr. Gladstone and Sir James Graham had been among his most determined opponents in the debate.[2] Moreover, not only were these men all adherents of a " non-interventionist " policy, they were also avowed opponents of a " pro-Turkish " policy. In addition, Lord Clarendon was as strong in his antipathy for the Turks as Aberdeen, and the Duke of Argyll, who was his devoted supporter, declared that " the integrity and independence of Turkish Empire " was a phrase " grotesquely inconsistent with the facts."[3] Finally, Sir William Molesworth was a Radical and a friend of Richard Cobden and therefore was expected to be in favour of a peaceful policy though he was notoriously consistent in his hostility to Russia.[4]

[1] Stanmore, *Aberdeen*, 31.
[2] Hansard, vol. cxi. 1401 ; cxii. 563 ff.
[3] Cp. Argyll, i. 441–465.
[4] Molesworth had offended his constituents in 1840 by holding " a peace meeting," to advocate alliance with France against Russia. Vide Fawcett, 32, and *D.N.B.*

Only four members of the Cabinet had voted in favour of Lord Palmerston in 1850. Their primary reason for doing so was that, as members of the Whig Government, they could not vote against their own Foreign Secretary. Lord Granville, who had been one of the chief promoters of the Exhibition in 1851, and had taken Palmerston's place after his dismissal in 1852, was always distinguished for his conciliatory attitude to foreign Powers.[1] Sir Charles Wood was absorbed in the reform of Indian administration and took little part in discussions of foreign affairs. Lord Lansdowne, as leader of the Whig Party in the Lords in 1850, had supported Palmerston, and was probably more in agreement with him than any other member of the Government. But he was an old man inclined to caution, and much under the influence of Aberdeen. As to Lord John Russell he had not approved of the policy of his Foreign Secretary, and had hesitated whether or not to seize the Don Pacifico incident as an opportunity to dismiss him.[2] A better opportunity had occurred a little later. Since then Palmerston's power had steadily grown, and Lord John's jealousy was no secret. It was highly unlikely that he would follow Palmerston's lead in foreign or any other kind of politics.

It seemed then that a new Don Pacifico incident would probably leave Lord Palmerston to fight a lonely battle.

[1] " Lord Granville was in later years the Foreign Minister after Bright's own heart, and his personal friend." In 1889, after Bright's death, he said in the House of Lords that in 1853 he had asked Lord Aberdeen why he did not invite Bright to join the Government—a remarkable proof of his pacific inclination. Trevelyan, *G.M.*, 230 and note.

[2] Vide above, 59.

2. The Newspapers.

Before the end of the eighteenth century Jeremy Bentham had decided that the success of political democracy depended on the establishment of a free newspaper Press. Having discovered the need of a new institution, he followed his usual method of procedure ; he drew up rules for its organization, converted his disciples to his suggestions, assisted at its birth, watched over its infancy and died before its frailty was manifest. When he first wrote there were only two kinds of journalist— the jackal of the politicians in power and the literary man on holiday. A regular journalist was a creature for contempt : while the occasional excursions into political controversy, indulged in by the feebler successors of Junius, did little to trouble the administrations of Pitt and Canning. When Bentham died the days of William Gifford were over as surely as those of Junius himself. The newspaper editor had achieved something of the dignity which Bentham had demanded for him as " President of the Public Opinion Tribunal."

Some small part of the change may be attributed to Bentham himself. He had founded *The Westminster Review*, and John Stuart Mill had edited it. Anthony Fonblanque who succeeded Leigh Hunt in the days when an epigram in *The Examiner* echoed like a pistol shot all over the kingdom, had been, like Black of *The Chronicle*, a disciple of Bentham and a friend of James Mill. *The Westminster Review* and *The Examiner* did much to keep the Utilitarian point of view before the minds of middle-class Radicals. Cobbett did still more for the profession of journalism by demonstrating the power of a continuous and courageous newspaper invective. For the Whigs, during their long period of political impotence, *The Edinburgh Review* alone provided a message and a hope. Brilliant writers who had hitherto scattered their energies in occasional articles, now formed themselves into a single body of journalists whose criticism only a Lord Eldon could ignore. Of the first editor of the *The Edinburgh Review*, Bagehot wrote : " Jeffrey was no everyday man. He invented the trade of editorship : before him an editor was a bookseller's dupe, he is now a distinguished functionary."[1]

The first great editors then were editors of periodicals. But with the widening of English political life after the Reform Bill, aided by the discovery of steam printing, the daily papers, hitherto of no great importance, began to assume leadership.[2] Periodicals took a second place. Their function was to sum up the gains of the past, not to form the opinions of the future. They ceased to be the centres of living controversy, and became the register of received opinion.

In the new era, *The Times*, already the greatest daily paper, quickly rose to a supreme position. In 1840 its daily circulation of 10,000 copies was more than twice that of any other paper. In 1852 it possessed a circulation of 40,000, while its nearest rival could only claim 7,000. Its influence was believed to be correspondingly great.

[1] Bagehot, i. 33.   Jeffrey's most able supporters were Sydney Smith, Brougham, and Horner.

[2] Daily papers still cost 5d.   It was not until the removal of the most burdensome of the taxes on knowledge in 1853 that a penny paper could appear.   In 1853 there was still a tax of 1/6 on every advertisement, an excise duty on paper and a newspaper stamp of a penny on each sheet.   This meant that the working-classes read only the Sunday papers.

Lord Clarendon wrote : " It is a well-known fact that *The Times* forms or guides or reflects—no matter which—the public opinion of England."

A large part of this success was due to the ability of its editors. John Barnes, who died in 1841, was called by Lord Lyndhurst " the most powerful man in England." Under his management *The Times* gained its curious " semi-official " position. But it was under his successor, John Thaddeus Delane, that it became admittedly the first paper in Europe.

Delane was an Irishman by descent and a country gentleman by instinct. In 1840, at the age of twenty-three, with an undistinguished degree, the reputation of being the best horseman in Oxford, and with no particular prospects, he entered the office of *The Times* of which his father was financial manager. In the following year John Barnes died and Mr. Walter, who had noticed unsuspected qualities in Delane, appointed him editor of the paper.[1]

Mr. John Walter gave the new editor a free hand. He was satisfied with his dividends, proud of the influence of his paper, and while these suffered no diminution, interfered but little in its management or policy. As editor of *The Times*, Delane found that he was the recipient of Ministerial confidences and in return was expected to support the Government. He accepted this position but greatly increased his independence by making friends with members of all political parties. He maintained a correspondence both with the Opposition and with the Ministry, and gained additional information from friends in France and other European countries. The " leaders " of *The Times* were usually based on his information and

[1] Cook, 8–10.

were written by brilliant men of his own choosing. They were read in every European Court and Cabinet, and foreign statesmen were apt to assume that the voice of *The Times* was the voice of the British public.

Delane's power is difficult to gauge. Clarendon was not sure whether *The Times* formed or guided or reflected public opinion. Perhaps it merely said what Delane and a few of his political friends thought at the moment! At any rate Delane did not suffer from the restrictions that bind the modern editor. He was not dictated to by advertisers, by party financiers, or by a millionaire proprietor with ambitions to become a popular dictator. Moreover, since he had no competitor to fear, Delane was able, for a time at least, to advocate a view offensive to a large number of his readers. When this occurred he received unstinted abuse, but the circulation of *The Times* did not diminish. It was commonly agreed that he could make or unmake Governments. He extracted apologies from the most powerful of statesmen and frequently received letters—almost of apology—from those whose conduct he had condemned. There was an undignified competition for his support. In 1852 Disraeli wrote four letters within forty-eight hours requesting the favour of *The Times* and received, by way of return, a cutting editorial describing him as an " inimitable illusionist " entertaining the public at the " pantomime of St. Stephens." [1]

Delane fully realized that power implied responsibility. From 1846 to 1852 he constantly opposed the methods of Palmerston in foreign affairs, even though *The Times* thereby " lost considerably in popularity." He particularly inveighed against

[1] Dasent, 80-5, 134-5 ; Cook, 59-60.

the national enthusiasm for Kossuth.[1] On one
matter, however, he agreed with the Liberals—
he had the liveliest detestation of Louis Napoleon.
The consequent hostility of *The Times* to the new
ruler of France led to a correspondence between
Lord Granville, the Foreign Secretary, on the one
hand, and Henry Reeve[2] and Delane on the other,
in which they discussed the duties of a newspaper
editor in days when an editor was still important.

The *coup d'état* of December 2nd, had been
consistently denounced in the strongest terms in
The Times. Lord Granville, who well knew that
a *de facto* Government must in course of time be
recognized by other Governments, wrote to Reeve,
thanking him for news of the situation in France,
but complaining that Napoleon was irritated and
annoyed beyond measure by the language of
The Times. " However such castigation may be
deserved," he said, " it will be a serious responsibility to goad him on to acts of violence which
may be seriously inconvenient to us."

Reeve, while admitting that two or three letters
had been written which " passed the bounds of
just commentary," defended his position : " The
responsibility of journalists is in proportion to the
liberty they enjoy. No moral obligation can be
graver. But their duties are not the same, I
think, as those of statesmen. To find out the
true state of affairs, to report them with fidelity,

---

[1] Dasent, i. 115–19; Morley, *Cobden*, ii. 71. So unpopular
was *The Times* made by its opposition to Kossuth that Cobden
wrote : " *The Times* has had a slap in the face which it will
not soon forget or forgive. It has been fairly cowed by the
universal execration it has brought upon itself. Yet what an absurd
position we are in. So completely dictated to and domineered
over by one newspaper that it requires a periodical revolt of the
whole people to keep the despot in tolerable order."

[2] Henry Reeve, Delane's best foreign leader writer, was the
editor of *Greville's Journal* and the translator of *de Tocqueville*.

to apply to them fixed and true principles of justice, humanity, and law, to inform, as far as possible, the very conscience of nations, and to call down the judgment of the world on what is false, or base, or tyrannical, appear to me to be the first duties of those who write. Those on whom the great part of political action devolves are necessarily governed by other rules."

Delane, to whom this letter was sent, heartily approved of Reeve's reply, and added that Lord Granville had "no necessary concern with the French people and its institutions except as they directly affect England. . . . Whatever he may feel as a private person, he, in his dealings with the French Government, is as much bound to suppress as we are to publish our opinions."[1]

The function of the journalist has perhaps never been more clearly put forward. The editor's task is two-fold : to publish the news and to comment on it in accordance with the " true principles of justice and humanity." He is, in fact, the " President of a Public Opinion Tribunal, pledged to no party, enlisted only in the service of the ' greatest happiness principle.' "[2] This was the ideal, but the true principles of justice and humanity were sometimes singularly elusive.

Delane was not given to introspection. If he had been, the events of 1853 might have suggested to him the need of some less simple formula. There were many complications. An initial difficulty was the conflict of loyalties. What if there should be, on some rare occasion, a discrepancy between the interests of England and the " true principles of justice and humanity ? " Again, what if the claims of friendship and inclination pointed one way and those of principle another ? Or, worst

[1] Reeve, i. 250–3.   [2] Vide above, 17.

of all, what if the turmoil of great events should bring no clear leading, but only doubt ?

All these questions arose. But for the journalist there was one even more difficult. Delane was confronted with the oldest problem of democracy : was he to give the public " what it wanted " or what he believed to be good for it ? If the latter, was the whole influence of *The Times* to be sacrificed by the persistent advocacy of a view which the country would not accept ? And if persuasion failed to bring his readers to reason, should the journalist betray his high calling " to report all the facts with fidelity " and think rather of the immediate and very pressing question of restraining them from acts of folly ?

The truth is that Delane's Benthamite theory broke down before the irrationality of his readers. Ultimately *The Times* depended on the public. If the public preferred what was not true, and wished to act in a manner which did not seem justified by the facts, the editor, in the last resort, was forced to choose between the ideal he had set himself and the retention of his influence by compromise.

So Delane, beginning in 1853 with a fear of Napoleon and a contempt for the Turk, an affection for Aberdeen and an abhorrence of Palmerston's policy, gradually found himself favouring an alliance with Napoleon whom he continued to distrust, advocating a war on behalf of Turkey, which he still believed to be the headquarters of " barbarism,"[1] increasingly diverging from Aberdeen, and finally taking a principal part in overthrowing him in favour of the popular hero, Lord

[1] As late as September he wrote to his correspondent in Constantinople, upbraiding him with expecting England to uphold barbarism (Turkey) against civilization (Russia) ! Vide below, 149.

Palmerston. Some part of this reversal of position was due, no doubt, to a considered change of opinion,[1] but no one who reads the story of 1853 can fail to see that it was the public which led and *The Times* which followed. Delane, like other conscientious men, first hesitated, then compromised, and finally retained his peace of mind by a whole-hearted conversion.

At the beginning of 1853, then, the Aberdeen Government was supported by *The Times*, and throughout the year there was a continual correspondence between Delane and Henry Reeve on the one side, and Aberdeen and Clarendon on the other. There was also a considerable indirect interchange of information and opinions between the Government and *The Times* through the medium of Charles Greville who constantly talked with Clarendon, the Duke of Newcastle, and Henry Reeve.[2]

The Government was also expecting support from *The Morning Chronicle* and its evening edition, *The Globe*. These papers had been both Liberal and Whig in the past, and had been used officially and unofficially by Russell and Palmerston.[3] But in 1848 *The Chronicle* was purchased

---

[1] This was certainly so in the winter of 1854, when Delane, urged on by the horrors of maladministration in the Crimea, directed the attack on the Aberdeen Government, which resulted in Palmerston's triumph of 1855. But even after the war had come Delane was not certain of its necessity. Vide below, 224.

[2] Vide Grev., vii. chaps. i–vi *passim*.

[3] *The Chronicle*, from its foundation Liberal and literary, was edited 1821–1843 by Black, a friend of John Stuart Mill. In 1834, its circulation had fallen to 1,000, and it was bought by a group of Whigs and regained a circulation of 6,000.

The Globe was edited by Colonel Robert Torrens, " the political economist." It had frequently been used for official purposes, e.g. Lord Granville used it in 1852. Granville, i. 55. For the use made of *The Globe* and *The Chronicle* by Lord John and Palmerston, vide Grant, ii. 73 ; *Cam. Hist.*, iii. 568 ; Fox Bourne, ii. 95, 169.

by a group of Peelites, including the Duke of New-castle and Sidney Herbert.[1]   Its new editor was John Douglas Cook, who had once been a reporter of Delane's,[2] and who was quite capable of acting independently of the paper's proprietors.[3] But far the most interesting figure on *The Chronicle* was Abraham Hayward, who engaged in an extensive correspondence with some of the most distinguished politicians and authors in England and France.[4]   He had been both energetic and useful in aiding Aberdeen during the formation of the Coalition in December 1852, and throughout 1853 did his best to support the Government.[5] But in the excitement of the Eastern Question the alliance between *The Chronicle* and the Government was destroyed and, by September, the editor and his most able contributor, William Harcourt, were becoming "bellicose."[6]   Aberdeen ceased to make use of *The Chronicle* and on September 14th, Hayward wrote to Sir J. Young, the Secretary for Ireland, complaining that the Government was not keeping its part of the bargain.

"Copies of public documents (the last dispatch of Lord Clarendon, published two days since, for example) are uniformly kept back from him and given to *The Times*. This is both unfair and impolitic. *The Chronicle* is the only morning paper that has uniformly supported the Govern-

[1] Stanmore, *Sidney Herbert*, i. 110 ff.; Fox Bourne, ii. 153–5.

[2] Escott, 231–2. Cook became editor of *The Saturday Review* in 1855.

[3] Hayward, ii. 200; Fox-Bourne, ii. 157.

[4] Louis Napoleon, Thiers, Macaulay. Sydney Smith, Lockhart, Lord Lansdowne, and Lord Lyndhurst were among his guests and correspondents.

[5] Hayward, i. 167.

[6] Ibid., 200; afterwards Sir William Harcourt. He had begun to write for *The Chronicle* while still an undergraduate at Cambridge in 1850. Gardiner, i. chap. iv.

ment, and *The Times* constantly turns against
it on the chance of gaining any stray ray of
popularity. It is an error to measure utility by
circulation. Every one of the leading papers is
read at all clubs and reading rooms. Its good
articles or arguments are reprinted or reproduced
in the provincial papers or worked up anew in the
shape of speeches, and always furnish topics for
the friends of the party it advocates. It thus
influences constituents and constituents command
votes. Look at the position of a party without
an organ during the Parliamentary recess. . . ."[1]
Hayward's warning went unheeded, and in 1854
the Peelite Party was left without any newspaper
support.[2]

The Aberdeen Cabinet represented the Whigs
and Radicals as well as the Peelites. At the
beginning of 1853, therefore, it was supported by
papers which were bitterly hostile to Lord Aberdeen
himself. *The Daily News*, edited by Knight Hunt
and famous for Harriet Martineau's contributions,
was inclined to support a Free Trade Government
which contained Sir William Molesworth.[3]

For similar reasons *The Manchester Guardian*,
already a judicial and carefully written paper,
naturally began by supporting the Coalition.[4]

[1] Hayward, ii., 189–90.

[2] *The Times* became its most powerful enemy in 1854, and *The
Chronicle* was again sold, November 1854. Hayward, ii. 225.

[3] The great days of *The Daily News* did not come until the Crimean
War had given it a great opportunity. At this time it stood for
Radical heterodoxy, Free Trade, and Palmerstonian foreign policy.
Douglas Jerrold wrote of it : " There is no God and Harriet Mar-
tineau is his prophet."

[4] *The Manchester Guardian* was published twice weekly. There
was no provincial daily paper, and provincial weeklies took their
news from London papers, and for the most part did little more
than summarize the views stated during the week by the London
organ of their party.

Even *The Morning Advertiser*, which was bought almost exclusively by keepers of Public Houses and Members of Parliament, and yet had the second circulation in the kingdom,[1] was inclined at the beginning of the session to tolerate a Cabinet of which Lord Palmerston was a member.

Lord Palmerston himself was not content with a general popularity in Whig and Radical newspapers. He preferred to have a paper which would owe allegiance to himself rather than to his party. *The Morning Chronicle* and *The Globe* were no longer available. But he had formed a new alliance of a more certain character.

The Morning Post, nominally a Tory paper, was the property of a staunch Conservative, Mr. Crompton. But the management was left in the hands of its editor, Peter Borthwick, who was an admirer and friend of Lord Palmerston. A steady correspondence was maintained between them, with the result that during the years 1848–52, *The Morning Post* alone was always satisfied with the conduct of English foreign policy.

In 1849, *The Morning Post's* attack on Austria and Russia had been directed by Palmerston. On one occasion, at least, he wrote a letter containing all the material necessary for a leading article.[2] In July 1850, we find him explaining his views on currency ; in August, discussing the stability of the Austrian Empire ; in October,

---

[1] Grant, ii. 60–2 ; Fox-Bourne, ii. 200. *The Morning Advertiser*, nicknamed "Gin and Gospel," was a liquor benefit society which insured publicans, paying them from 7s. to 10s. a week in time of difficulty. It was not taken in by private houses but had a circulation in 1850 of 5,000, in 1853 of 7,000, in 1854, 8,000, in Public Houses, coffee shops, and clubs. It was strongly Radical until the Licensing Act of 1868. James Grant, its editor at this time, was a Scotch Presbyterian, a hymn writer, and author of *The Newspaper Press*.

[2] Glenesk, 132.

deriding the " Papal aggression " ; and in December, speculating on the character of the young Emperor of Austria and the nature of the Government of Louis Napoleon. In January 1852, he expressed satisfaction that *The Post* had not attacked the Prince on the occasion of his dismissal in December 1851, because it was " less evil for the country that any number of Ministers should be sent to the right-about than that the good will and attachment of the people to the sovereign and her consort should be impaired." He urged that it was " wretched nonsense to imagine that the French do not contemplate an invasion of England as an attempt to be made in possible contingencies, and that it was therefore our business to prepare ourselves without panic." [1]

During the crisis of 1851, the special correspondent of *The Morning Post* at Paris was the editor's own son, Algernon Borthwick.[2] He had made many friends in Paris, among whom was Louis Napoleon himself. At the time of the *coup d'état* he interviewed the Emperor and sent home an account to *The Morning Post*, based on his own words.[3] His constant letters to Peter Borthwick were well informed and amusing. They were also entirely favourable to Louis Napoleon and enthusiastic in their support of Palmerston's foreign policy. It was not then surprising that both Palmerston and Louis Napoleon expressed approbation of Algernon's work. Mrs. Borthwick, too, was delighted. In February she wrote to Algernon : " We went to Lady Palmerston's last Saturday. Your papa had two hours with him on Sunday and showed him your last long letter.

---

[1] Glenesk, 133–6.
[2] Algernon Borthwick became Lord Glenesk in 1895.
[3] Glenesk, 97–8.

Lord P. said it was very interesting and very true."
The great man even declared that Algernon was
"the only man—next to himself—fit to be Foreign
Secretary." [1] Louis Napoleon contented himself
with warmly thanking Peter Borthwick for "the
impartial view *The Morning Post* has taken of
French affairs." [2]

In the spring of 1852, Peter Borthwick retired
and Algernon returned from Paris to take his
father's place.[3] He continued his intimate connection with the French Government. He saw
the French ambassador, Walewski, "every day,"
and, according to one account, received money
in exchange for his support.[4] Lord Malmesbury,
then Foreign Secretary, perhaps naturally complained when "an article in *The Morning Post*
from its correspondent in Paris" retailed "nearly
every word" of his last conversation with
Walewski.

The Ministry, of which Malmesbury was a member, approached the editor himself. A certain
"Mr. P. sent by a member of the Government,"
called upon Algernon Borthwick and offered
Government information in return for the support
of *The Morning Post*. He explained that the
Tories were "dissatisfied with *The Herald* and were
desirous of securing a valuable organ and in the
cheapest manner possible." The offer was refused.
The Morning Post was already bought. Moreover,
Algernon Borthwick had no desire for a new

---

[1] Glenesk, 72–3 ; cp. Ashley, i. 287.

[2] Ibid., 96.

[3] Peter Borthwick died at the end of 1852 and Algernon, who
had already directed *The Morning Post* for some months, became
official editor. Glenesk, 123.

[4] Malmesbury, i. 362. "Sent for Walewksi. He confessed that
the French Government paid *The Morning Post*, and that he saw
Borthwick, the editor, every day."

alliance, however tactfully offered. He agreed
with his father's summary of the situation : " The
Government may communicate with you directly
if it seems good to them, but we cannot sacrifice
that independence of party and that strong
adherence to principle which constitutes the
character and the chief value of a newspaper." [1]

During 1852, the Derby Ministry grew increasingly " dissatisfied with *The Herald* and its evening
edition, *The Standard.*" [2] The violence of their
support did not atone for their lack of discrimina-
tion. Ministers did their best to disavow any
connection with such unwise friends. Disraeli,
in spite of his former rebuff, wrote to Delane,
thanking him for such support as *The Times* had
given to the new Ministry, and apologizing for
the fact that a " quasi-authentic version of the
(Queen's) Speech" had appeared in *The Morning
Herald.* "*The Morning Herald* is not my organ
and I trust never will be ; in fact, I never wish
to see my name in its columns. But I'm bound
to tell you, because I know it, that the version in
question proceeded from no member of the Government. A guest of Lord Derby, I suspect to be
the traitor—not, however, a traitor in office." [3]

On a later and more serious occasion he again
disclaimed all responsibility for the behaviour of
the Tory papers.[4] He wrote to Mr. Ponsonby
that " far from having much influence over the
papers you mention, I not only have none, but
they are my secret or my avowed foes . . .
The truth is, great errors exist as to the influence
of party leaders over what are esteemed party

[1] Glenesk, 118.
[2] They were owned and edited by Edward Baldwin.
[3] Dasent, i. 148.
[4] During the attack on Prince Albert in January 1854, vide below,
214.

journals." "Holding them by no proprietary tie, and indebted to us for no pecuniary aid, they look only to their circulation, and will follow up any cry which they believe tends to increase their sale." [1]

If in 1849, Disraeli had found the state of the Tory Press "deplorable," in 1853 he found it intolerable. "It seems," he complained, "that the whole ability of the country is arrayed against us, and the rising generation is half ashamed of a cause which would seem to have neither wit nor reason to sustain and adorn it." He, therefore, proposed to found a weekly paper, and himself to supervise its production. The Tory Party was no longer to lack either wit or reason.[2]

The first number of *The Press* appeared on May 7, 1853. The editorial, written by Disraeli himself, was a masterpiece of invective, and throughout the whole period of the Coalition Ministry there was no relaxation either in the acidity of his wit or in the virulence of his vituperation. It was well known, during this period, that he wrote in almost every number, though he made elaborate and sometimes amusing efforts to hide his identity.[3] Lord Aberdeen, against whom his bitterest sallies were directed, had no difficulty in detecting their origin. Disraeli's wit, occasional in his novels, mordant in his speeches, and deliberately cruel in his journalism, is everywhere unmistakably

---

[1] Buckle, iii. 530.

[2] Vide ibid., iii. 489–94, for a full account of the origin of *The Press*. Disraeli continued his intimate connection with it until February 1856, and retained his ownership until 1858. It achieved at its best a circulation of 3,500, but its finances were always somewhat troubled.

[3] Ibid., iii. 501. Disraeli, for instance, cricitized one of his own speeches as "in our opinion much too long and savouring somewhat of the Yankee school of rhetoric."

his own. The Premier was not unconscious of its sting and was at length driven to complain in the House of the " malignity and misrepresentations " to which he had been subjected. Perhaps the fact that amid the misrepresentations there was sometimes a sharp edge of truth added vehemence to Aberdeen's protest.[1]

In 1853, then, the Tory point of view was expressed in the daily commonplaces of *The Herald* and in the weekly brilliance of *The Press*. Among the other Tory weeklies the most interesting is *John Bull*, which, though no longer enlivened by the humour of Theodore Hook, still retained the gaiety of complete irresponsibility. *John Bull* was always outspoken, and its fear of invasion from France was only surpassed by its dread of the Roman religion. Equally devout, but more cautious, was *The Guardian*, which came nearest to expressing the religious convictions of Mr. Gladstone.

Among the Radicals there was still a strong body of Nonconformist pacifists. They had no daily paper. Both *The Times* and *The Manchester Guardian* reported their meetings at length and offered them careful criticism. A monthly paper, *The Herald of Peace*, expressed the views of the more extreme section of the Peace Society.

An examination of the papers so far described would give us a fair estimate of the views of the voting population. It would exclude that great mass of citizens who were unrepresented in the House of Commons. Working-class people could not afford a daily paper at fivepence, even if it had been intended to interest them. The great Chartist papers of the 'forties had died with the movement which gave them birth. But we may

[1] Hansard, 31/3/54.

find in two widely read Sunday papers an expression of the views of the thinking section of the working-class.

The Weekly Dispatch, famous for its articles by " Publicola," was Radical in its views, inclined towards Republicanism, and was unabashed by charges of atheism.[1] It was not seriously interested in foreign affairs but was largely devoted to the cause of distressed operatives, to police news, and to the abolition of the remaining " taxes on knowledge." *Reynolds's Weekly*,[2] on the other hand, was always well informed on foreign policy, and enthusiastically supported Kossuth and other heroes of European democracy. Unlike *The Weekly Dispatch*, also, it was well printed and never dull. It was definitely Chartist in its outlook, and its readers were probably former adherents of Feargus O'Connor and *The Northern Star*.

We have now covered almost the whole field of the English newspaper Press. In times of excitement, however, we may find indications of opinion outside the newspapers. Pamphlets appear ; public meetings are called ; broadsides and popular songs display political sentiment where reasoned opinion is commonly lacking. In an analysis of public opinion, therefore, we must regard these as symptoms. They will be, in some degree, a test of the success of newspaper propaganda.

It should be clear from this account of the position of the English Press in 1853 that articulate public opinion was likely to favour Palmerston rather than Aberdeen. On Aberdeen's side were

[1] Its circulation in 1855 was 38,000. For the history of its struggle with *The Times* in 1840, under the leadership of James Horner and William Johnson Fox, vide Fox-Bourne, ii. 103.

[2] Reynolds was a Chartist who had taken to journalism and the writing of doubtful fiction. His *Weekly* was founded in 1850 at the cost of fourpence. Its circulation in 1855 was about 50,000.

The Times and *The Chronicle*. Against him were almost all the other English newspapers even though, at first, some of them supported his Government. On Palmerston's side was the general popularity of his policy and the charm of his personality. There was also one newspaper directly inspired by him. The alliance between Palmerston and *The Morning Post* was no secret, though the degree of its intimacy was a matter of guesswork. *The Post*, therefore, had an importance far greater than its circulation would at first suggest ; for it early betrayed the disunity of the Cabinet. From the time when the divergence between *The Post* and *The Times* first became obvious, the cause of *The Post* was taken up with enthusiasm by all who loved Palmerston or hated Aberdeen. Party rivalry, Liberal sentiment, and natural pugnacity all compelled a simultaneous attack. This attack had no connection with the merits of any particular issue. It so happened that the Eastern Question provided the material for the struggle, but any other question on which Palmerston and Aberdeen were known to differ would have served the same purpose.

We are now in a position to examine the interaction of these factors during 1853.

CHAPTER V

" THE SIMPLE DUTIES OF A PEACEMAKER "

(January–June)

1. The Cabinet and Lord Stratford.
(January–March)

In January 1853 the prospects of the new Ministry seemed excellent. No one could doubt the ability of its members and Lord Aberdeen's friends were delighted with his triumphant achievement of a task which had been pronounced impossible. Lord John was at length satisfied and agreed to postpone the introduction of his Reform Bill until the following winter. Finance seemed the most likely source of danger. Mr. Disraeli would undoubtedly seek revenge for his last year's defeat, and rumour had it that Mr. Gladstone's Budget was destined to be a bold one. But, if eloquence could persuade the House of Commons that the differentiation of the income tax was contrary to the Divine plan, the Ministry was safe.[1]

Foreign affairs were troublesome, but not, for the moment, dangerous. The agitation against Louis Napoleon was not abated. There was a rumour that he was about to seize the Channel Islands, and in February Lord Palmerston wrote

---

[1] Mr. Gladstone was successful, and it was largely due to his personal scruples that differentiation between earned and unearned incomes was postponed till the twentieth century.

to Sidney Herbert that, in his opinion, the danger was a real one. " In the present state of things the French might by steam easily throw a large body of troops into the Channel Islands. . . . The Duke of Wellington, who was a good judge of strategy, attached the greatest importance to these islands as a military position. The best thing would be to fortify them all. . . ." [1] Mr. Sidney Herbert, however, considered that the institution of a military camp at Chobham and a grand naval review would be sufficient to dispel the popular excitement.[2]

In the East, a dispute between Turkey and Austria, who had sent Count Leinigen to demand the Turkish evacuation of Bosnia, did not at first seem to affect England, and even when Russia complained that the Porte was not carrying out her obligations in the " Holy Places," the question was not considered important enough to become

[1] Stanmore, *Sidney Herbert*, i. 179.
[2] For the effect of Chobham Camp on the panic the following popular ballad is suggestive :

"CHOBHAM CAMP (1850).

" From Spain and France the mob will dance,
　　To Chobham Heath so hearty,
And on the ground I 'll bet a pound,
　　The Emperor Bonaparte,
Would like to be, our Queen to see,
　　And gaily to behold her,
Eyes left and right in armour bright
　　View England's gallant soldiers.

In pleasant June, such glorious tunes
　　On Chobham Heath will cheer us,
And ev'ry nation in the world,
　　In time of war shall fear us.
Britannia's deeds proud France may read,
　　Victory all times did crown her,
If Boney comes to Chobham Camp
　　We'll show him English power."

" Chobham Camp," a ballad preserved in the British Museum.

a matter of Cabinet discussion. The news that
the Tsar had again expressed his view that Turkey
was a " sick man " did not alarm Lord John or
Aberdeen : the dissolution of the Ottoman Empire
had been envisaged in the protocol of 1844 and
was expected by most competent authorities. When
it was announced that the Tsar was sending Prince
Menschikoff on an extraordinary mission to Constantinople, Lord John was assured by Brunmow,
the Russian ambassador in London, that the
Tsar had no intention of making new demands but
merely desired to persuade Turkey to carry out
her obligations under existing treaties. It was
clear, however, that a " mere chargé d'affaires " was
no longer competent to watch over English interests in the East and Sir Stratford-Canning was
given a peerage and once more dispatched as
our ambassador to the Porte. The decision was
not made without hesitation. Lord Stratford was
not indeed an ordinary ambassador.

Among the many undecided questions of English
administration not the least important was the
relationship of our ambassadors abroad with the
Ministry in power. The Cabinet depended on
the foreign embassies for much of its information,
not only of the official proceedings of foreign
Governments, but also of those unofficial conversations which form the hidden substance of
diplomacy. Further, the Cabinet relied on the
embassy to communicate its views and intentions
to foreign Governments. Theoretically, no doubt,
the relationship between ambassador and Foreign
Minister was simply that of master and confidential
servant. But complications arose. The ambassador might hold personal views which conflicted
with the official ones of his Cabinet. The distinction between private and public is often hard

to find, and opinions, expressed unofficially, some-times assume more importance than Imperial statements.

Even in Paris difficulties had arisen, and a change of Ministry was sometimes found to necessitate a change of ambassador.[1] In the case of a distant capital, to which the telegraphic system had not yet reached, the ambassador necessarily exercised a wide personal discretion. How independent an embassy could be under these circumstances had been fully demonstrated by Sir Stratford-Canning in the matter of the refugees in 1849.[2]

Lord Stratford's position at the Porte was of a peculiar nature. His ability, his experience, and his authority were unique. He had been ambassador at Constantinople five times and had already spent forty years cutting the diplomatic knots of Europe. He was fully alive to the evils of Turkish misrule and set himself to encourage reform by the establishment of English influence. Turkey he treated as a wilful child to be guided, cajoled, rewarded, bullied, and, if necessary, punished. He offered protection and expected obedience. He had his own policy for Turkey and knew it to be the right one. He did not compromise. For expediency, Mr. Lane Poole tells us, he had no respect: "Right and wrong he knew, but the expedient was a middle course which he refused to recognize."[3] Right was clearly on the side of Reshid Pasha whose party was pledged to reforms of which Lord Stratford approved.

[1] Cf. correspondence on the recall of Lord Normanby in January 1852. Granville, i. 55.

[2] Lane Poole, ii. 191 *seq.* The telegraphic system had extended only as far as Vienna; cp. *Cam. Hist.*, ii. 346, 351; Maxwell, ii. 27. The record speed for a messenger was sixteen days in 1849. Vide Lane Poole's romantic footnote, ii. 194.

[3] Ibid., 56–7.

With a clear conscience, therefore, he sought by all the forces of intrigue by night, and intimidation by day, to secure success for his favourite Minister.[1]

This high-minded policy led him to engage in a continuous running warfare with the Tsar, whose influence at the Porte was in a direction opposite to his own. Their enmity was notorious, and on one occasion the Tsar had taken the unusual step of refusing to accept Lord Stratford as ambassador at St. Petersburg. Some men might have allowed their policy to be affected by this treatment. But Lord Stratford was no ordinary man. " He felt," we are told, " that it belonged to him to sustain the dignity of the Queen by every act ; that he was the embodiment of the Crown in the eyes of the Court to which he was accredited ; that a slight offered to him was an insult to his sovereign. This high and noble feeling," his biographer adds, " had nothing personal in it." [2]

Human motives, however, are seldom simple, and those who worked with Lord Stratford were not always equally confident. The Home Government at any rate would have preferred more obedience and less highmindedness. Lord Aberdeen had already found difficulty in working with so independent an ambassador, and on one occasion spoke of the need of " bringing him to his senses." Sir James Graham, a few months later, declared that, " notwithstanding the peremptory order to the contrary," Lord Stratford was " quite capable of advising the Turks to be refractory." This

[1] For a description of his methods by an excellent contemporary observer, vide Layard, ii. 56–7. Cp. Lane Poole, chap. xvii.

[2] Lane Poole, ii. 57. Lane Poole's judgment of Lord Stratford seems to come direct from Kinglake, but the latter does, in one place, admit that his hero was, after all, " an imperfect Christian." Kinglake, i. 119.

was the opinion not only of members of the Cabinet but also of other ambassadors.[1]

If opinions of this sort could be held before definite evidence of his disobedience was forthcoming it is easy to understand why Lord Aberdeen wrote to Lord John that " it will be necessary to be very careful in preparing instructions for Lord Stratford."[2] Clearly he would have preferred not to make the appointment. Yet the difficulties in the way of refusing to nominate Stratford seemed greater. He was indisputably able, popular at home, and unique in his influence with the reforming party in Turkey. Above all the cordial dislike that existed between him and the Tsar was well known : a refusal to send Lord Stratford would have been interpreted at home as an unwarranted concession to the Tsar. Was it better to offend the Tsar or public opinion ? There was as yet no reason to believe that the negotiations were dangerous, and the Tsar was less menacing than the daily paper. Lord John sent Stratford, and the Government had made its first concession to public opinion.[3]

It so happens that some curious evidence is accessible which helps to explain Lord Stratford's persistent popularity with the Press. Mr. Layard who long worked with the British Embassy at Constantinople, and who first went out as a newspaper correspondent, writes as follows : [4] " It was of much importance to Sir Stratford that he should have the support of the English and European

---

[1] Maxwell, ii. 16–19. Vide Letters from Lord Cowley and others, below, 138. Cp. Layard, ii. 70–1.

[2] Walpole, ii. 178.

[3] Lane Poole, ii. 226–7. Stratford's biographer uses the language of hyperbole at this point. " There arose a universal cry for Lord Stratford to return and protect his ancient ward. Ministers bowed to the necessity."

[4] Layard, ii. 123–4.

Press. My friendship with Mr. Longworth, who was then correspondent of *The Morning Post*, and my acquaintance with many other newspaper correspondents, enabled me to hold out good hopes to him that I should be able to obtain from them that support and induce them to write favourably of his policy, and to put forward any views with regard to it which he might desire should be generally known. I was as good as my word. . . . The unanimity of so large a portion of the public Press in approving the policy of Sir Stratford-Canning greatly strengthened his position and influence in Constantinople, and secured for him the support of public opinion in England. He was thus able to carry out many of his own views, which were not always in accordance with those of Lord Aberdeen and the English Government, and to compel the Porte to adopt measures and to introduce reforms which he conscientiously believed would tend to promote the well-being of the Ottoman Empire and especially of its Christian populations, and, at the same time, the interests of England. There was thus a chorus of praise of the English ambassador in the European Press, and I learnt by experience how much the success and reputation of a diplomatist may depend upon his skill in obtaining the support of newspaper correspondents and their incessant and exaggerated approval of all that he says and does. The public can only be guided by reports coming from such quarters, and is only too ready to believe everything that is written concerning a man who is so universally commended."

2. The Sailing of the Fleet.
(The Cabinet—March–June)

IN March, Clarendon took Lord John's place at the Foreign Office. The new Minister stood, in many ways, in sharp contrast to Lord John. He was suave where Lord John was acrimonious, and his suavity was most remarkable in his dispatches—which was just where Lord John's bluntness was most disconcerting. The only disadvantage was that, whereas Lord John's meaning was always terribly obvious, it was sometimes difficult to be sure just where Clarendon's "limpid flow of delicate words" had taken you.[1] He worked indefatigably though with curious irregularity. His skill in diplomatic compromise made relations smooth, at least for the time, not only between nations but also between Cabinet personalities. "He is," writes Algernon Cecil, "one of the very few men, perhaps the only man, with a right to be called a *diplomate de carrière*, who ever held the seals of the Foreign Office."[2]

On assuming office, Clarendon found that the Eastern Question had assumed a new and menacing aspect. Russia was said to be gathering troops on the borders of the Principalities in support of demands which were not confined to the question of the Holy Places.

Prince Menschikoff's behaviour was undoubtedly arrogant and Fuad Effendi's enforced resignation suggested that French interests at the Porte might suffer. Louis Napoleon, therefore, ordered his fleet to sail to Salamis, and Colonel Rose, who before Lord Stratford's arrival was in command at the Embassy, invited Admiral Dundas to advance in company with the French fleet.

On the arrival of the dispatches from Rose and Dundas, Lord Clarendon, having sent for Lord John, also summoned Palmerston in the hope that this deferential treatment would "keep him

---

[1] Bagehot, *Biographical Studies.*
[2] *Cam. Hist.,* iii. 584.

in a good humour " [1] ; Sir James Graham was also at hand. The question of the advance of our fleet was therefore discussed by Aberdeen, Palmerston, John Russell, Graham, and Clarendon. They decided to reply to Colonel Rose that Admiral Dundas had been wise in refusing to co-operate with Napoleon, whose action seemed unnecessary and provocative.

This pacific policy was adopted by the five men who were throughout all the subsequent negotiations really responsible for England's attitude. On this occasion a decision was reached without great difficulty, but the differences of outlook and temperament which were ultimately to wreck the harmony of the Cabinet were already discernible. All were agreed that it was a primary duty to preserve peace. All were agreed that Russia must not be allowed to occupy Constantinople and that Turkey must, if possible, be maintained there for some time longer. But they differed as to the right method of preserving the peace, as to the real intentions of Russia, and as to the state and merits of the Ottoman Empire.

Lord John Russell and Lord Palmerston believed that a bold policy of coercion was the right one in regard to Russia. In 1849 the Tsar had resigned his claim upon the Hungarian refugees in Turkey in face of English determination. They believed he would resign his new demands under similar pressure. The very mention of Russian demands at Constantinople was enough to recall the picture of 1849. When Lord Clarendon communicated the situation to Lord John, " he got an answer from him, full of very wild talk of strong measures to be taken, and a fleet sent to the Baltic to make peremptory demands on the Emperor of Russia. This, however, he [Clarendon] took no notice of,

[1] Grev., vii. 56.

and did not say one word to Aberdeen about it, quietly letting it drop, and accordingly he heard no more about it. . . ."

Lord Palmerston entertained the same views, but was more cautious. At the meeting " he did not say much and acquiesced in Aberdeen's prudent and reserved intentions," but from a few words that casually escaped him, it was clear that he would have been " ready to join in more stringent and violent measures if they had been proposed."[1]

Lord Aberdeen was altogether opposed to such measures on behalf of Turkey, and Lord Clarendon and Sir James Graham were in agreement with him. To them the Eastern Question recalled quite a different set of images ; the persecution of Christians, the incident of Navarino, and the freedom of Greece. In 1827, a British public had rejoiced to aid in the spoiling of the Turk, and Aberdeen could remember that Lord John Russell had been glad of the successes of Russia and Lord Palmerston had asked why the Turk should remain at Constantinople. Moreover, he knew the Tsar's vanity, and was convinced that " assurances of prompt and effective aid in the approach of danger, given by us to the Porte, would in all probability produce war."[2]

At the outset, therefore, Lord Aberdeen believed that attempts to coerce the Tsar would merely exasperate him, while Lord Palmerston thought that they would intimidate him. This difference of opinion was closely connected with a second. Lord Palmerston believed that under Lord Stratford's management Turkey would reform and continue to exercise its " progressively liberal system " at Constantinople.[3] Lord Aberdeen admitted that " to allow Russia to rejuvenate the

[1] Grev., vii. 56.   [2] Stanmore, *Aberdeen*, 70–1.   [3] Ashley, ii. 37.

sick man of Europe would be too expensive,"
but thought that to allow Lord Stratford to act
as doctor was almost equally dangerous.   Moreover, he did not believe that any reform of the
" crapulous barbarians [1] " was possible, and was
only in agreement with other Cabinet Ministers
when he declared that " to talk of the independence
and integrity of the Turkish Empire was absurd."
" Every day," he said, " renders more certain the
impossibility of any European sympathy with a
system founded on ignorance and ferocity." [2]

When towards the end of April the Eastern
Question became a matter of discussion in the
Cabinet, these differences did not at first appear.
" There was not," wrote Argyll, recalling the
period many years afterwards, " a shadow of
difference among us as to the course which it was
our duty to pursue."   The duty of England was
to adhere to the principles of the former treaties ; it
was " simply the duty of a peacemaker."   Further,
all were agreed that we should be in a better position as peacemaker if we were acting in co-operation
with France and, if possible, the German Powers.[3]
Success depended on Austrian support.

Difficulty, however, soon arose in the administration of this simple office of peacemaker.   In
the first place was it only Russia who was breaking
the peace ?   Lord Aberdeen, at any rate, thought
Napoleon's action in dispatching the fleet unneces-
sarily provocative, but there could be no doubt
that the Tsar was endangering the peace when he
mobilized troops on the frontiers of the Principalities, and at length, after a number of threatening
Notes, actually gave Gortschatoff orders to cross

[1] Reeve, i. 288, quoting Lord Aberdeen.
[2] Stanmore, *Aberdeen*, 85.
[3] Argyll, i. 443 *seq.*

8

the Pruth. These actions were particularly irritating because doubt existed, as it still exists, whether Prince Menschikoff had really been, in Nesselrode's words, only attempting to " maintain the rights which had existed for ages,"[1] or whether, on the other hand, Lord Stratford was right in declaring that " the guarantee required by Russia was objectionable to the Porte on grounds of real danger to its independence and . . . went far beyond the treaties existing." [2]

In view of the fact that the matter at issue was one of diplomatic verbiage and that Russia had taken certain embarrassing and hostile steps, what was the just attitude of a peacemaker ? There were two possible attitudes. The first was Lord Aberdeen's : To continue to negotiate in conjunction with other Powers but without ourselves taking any hostile steps which would retard our freedom to withdraw if our part as peacemaker failed. The second was Lord Palmerston's : To utilize the fleet as a menace against the aggressor and thus enforce peace by presenting a bold front on behalf of Turkey. Possibly either policy, if wholeheartedly adopted, would have succeeded in preserving peace.

Unfortunately neither policy was adopted : a compromise was reached at every discussion. When Prince Menschikoff delivered an ultimatum and left the Porte, the threats of Russia were met by a Note to Lord Stratford empowering him to call up the fleet if necessary. Lord Aberdeen opposed this policy. " It is," he said, " a fearful power to place in the hands of any Minister, involving as it does, the question of peace and war." [3]

---

[1] *E.P.*, 231. Count Nesselrode to Sir H. Seymour.
[2] Ibid., 215.
[3] *Correspondence*, Letter to Sir James Graham, 1/6/53.

A little later, when the Tsar seemed about to enter the Principalities, Lord Palmerston proposed that such an action should be considered a *casus belli*.[1] He was not supported and withdrew. A middle course was adopted. The fleet advanced to the entrance of the Dardanelles and Lord Clarendon, at the same time, wrote a forcible letter to Lord Stratford desiring him to explain to Turkey that our support depended on drastic reforms being carried out on behalf of the Christians under Ottoman rule, since the only real security for Turkey lay " in enlisting the feelings of the Christians on its behalf. The Turk must decide between the maintenance of an erroneous religious principle and the loss of the sympathy and support of the allies." [2]

This compromise between Lord Aberdeen's position and Lord Palmerston's was the work of Lord Clarendon. Without Aberdeen's confidence in the Tsar, or Palmerston's belief in Stratford, he acted as mediator. It was a fatal mediation. By this middle policy England was as much committed to support Turkey as she would have been if Palmerston's policy had been adopted outright. Lord Aberdeen realized that this hesitating encouragement of the Porte was dangerous. He wrote to Clarendon : " If we have good reason to expect an attack on Constantinople, and are disposed to quarrel with Russia for the protection of the Turks, we ought to approach the capital or rather to enter the Black Sea, by which means any naval move on the part of Russia could be effectually stopped. The only effect of such half measures as are recommended would be to release the Emperor of Russia from the obligations which he has voluntarily contracted towards us without accomplishing our

---

[1] Grev., vii. 72.   [2] *E.P.*, 293, 24/6/53.

own object. I think our best prospect of success is to be found in the union of the four Powers, and in their firm but friendly representations at St. Petersburg." [1]

In view of such words as these it has naturally been asked why Aberdeen and Clarendon allowed themselves to be entangled in a quarrel on behalf of Turkey. The answer is not that Palmerston fought for his opinion ; that a heated debate was followed by a vote on a compromise suggested by Clarendon. Nothing of this sort occurred. There was never any voting [2] ; if there had been, the Cabinet would almost all have voted with the Prime Minister. There was scarcely any debating. " Palmerston urged his proposal perseveringly, but not disagreeably," wrote Lord Aberdeen a little later, and he seems to have adopted this attitude from the beginning. Lord Clarendon provides us with the real explanation in a letter to Lord Aberdeen on May 31st. " I recommend this (i.e. the dispatch of the fleets) as *the least measure that will satisfy public opinion* and save the Government from shame hereafter, if, as I firmly believe, the Russian hordes pour into Turkey from every side. It may do some good to ourselves, which should not be our last consideration." [3]

There was no need for Palmerston to put forward his position " disagreeably " : the newspapers in the country were doing that for him. Clarendon always declared that the public would not support a European war unless every avenue of peace had been exhausted. Aberdeen tried to think as little as possible about what the public would do. Palmerston, on the other hand, knew that the public would at first be delighted if war broke out

[1] Stanmore, *Aberdeen*, 224. [2] Argyll, i. 455.
[3] Maxwell, ii. 25. (My italics.)

with Russia. Not that he wanted war. He had his own method of satisfying the public. He liked to steer " the ship of State in a high wind, on a rough sea, with every stitch of canvas on her that she could carry," [1] and then, at the last moment, to avoid the final collision by a dexterous turn of the wheel which left his colleagues gasping and the country satisfied. But he could not pilot the ship at the moment and it was with horror that Aberdeen and Clarendon found themselves in a position which would exactly have suited their colleague. The Coalition depended on an uncertain majority in the Commons ; members of Parliament were dependent on their constituents and were easily affected by the newspapers ; if the Coalition was defeated, a more warlike Government would follow. It was, therefore, necessary to adopt " the least measure that would satisfy public opinion "—however little commendable the measure itself might appear.

It is now time to discover what Lord Clarendon meant by " public opinion " at this stage, and ask why it demanded the sailing of the fleet.

3. A Change of Picture.

(Public Opinion—January–June)

The agitation against Napoleon III, which had persisted without intermission since the *coup d'état*, was at its height in January 1853. The conviction that he was about to invade England was as strong as ever. It was rumoured that he intended first to descend upon the Channel Islands or possibly upon Belgium. *John Bull* foresaw an even worse danger. Louis Napoleon, " surrounded by parasites, pimps, and prostitutes," might at any moment " invade England or Ireland, under

[1] Strachey, 152.

the banner of the Pope, as the chosen champion
of the ' Catholic Faith.' " Did not the Government contain Catholics in its subordinate offices
and those dangerously near to Catholicism in the
highest positions ? Was it not plain, asked an
editorial, that Napoleon would be " able to obtain
whatever information he chose through the intervention of the Popish priesthood, whose tools—
if not its hands, at least its eyes and its ears, are
now installed in official situations ? " " Would
not Mr. Gladstone combine with Monsell the
Jesuit pervert, Keogh, the Pope's pioneer, in all
which makes Popery abhorrent and Protestantism
ridiculous ? " [1]

Other papers were scarcely less vehement.
The Morning Post, true to its alliance, took up
a solitary stand on behalf of the Emperor.[2] Delane,
too, though still distrustful of Napoleon's intentions,
had realized a few months before that the time
for abuse of an established monarch and possible
ally was past. " I think," he wrote, " that we
have picked that bone pretty bare, and shall do
ourselves, instead of him, injury if we continue
to abuse him." In January, therefore, *The Times*
complimented Napoleon on his marriage, and
expressed the hope that the Empress Eugenie
would find the throne of France more comfortable
than " the last aspirer to her perilous position." [3]
But there were a few who thought that greater
efforts should be made to allay the agitation.

[1] *John Bull*, 1/1/53. Monsell and Keogh were Irish Catholics
whom Aberdeen had given posts, in order to please the Irish Tenant
League. Keogh was Solicitor-General for Ireland.

[2] Cp. especially 22/1/53.

[3] 21/1/53. Delane himself went to Paris to witness Napoleon's
marriage, but though ordering this change of policy he still believed
Napoleon dangerous if only because of the popularity war would
bring. Dasent, i. 147–54.

To patronize Napoleon was scarcely a sufficient remedy. At the beginning of the year, therefore, Cobden wrote that the object of the Peace Society should be " to beat down this most wicked spirit toward France." He himself was composing a pacifist pamphlet,[1] attempting to prove that the war of 1792 was provoked, not by France, but by England, and suggesting that the " invasion scare " might again provoke France against her will. His argument was reinforced at a Peace Conference held in Edinburgh, and received wide but uniformly unflattering attention in the Press. *The Manchester Guardian*, among the most sober of his critics, spoke of " the hopeless task of convincing the people of England that they may make themselves perfectly easy as to the designs of the very unscrupulous gentleman whose iron will and inscrutable purposes wield the vast aggressive power of France, who has got an army of 400,000 men . . . and who is straining every nerve to accumulate a large force of powerful steamships which will enable him in a single night to transport forty or fifty thousand of these troops to the gates of Portsmouth or Sheerness." [2] The task did seem hopeless. The propaganda of the Peace Society apparently worked according to a " law of reversed effort : " the stronger their advocacy of peace, the more bitter was the hostility they aroused. Suddenly there came a change. Was the leaven really working ? " Gallophobia," declared *The Herald of Peace*, " is passing." England was returning to common sense, and one writer, after quoting the opinions of many great authorities, ranging from Montesquieu to the Duke

[1] 1792 *and* 1853 *in Three Letters*; *Political Writings*, vol. i; Hobson, 93 *seq.*

[2] 29/1/53. Cp. *M.P.*, 28/1/53 ; *Blackwood's*, vol. 73, 364.

of Wellington, found that Lord John Russell, in a moment of inspiration had been nearest the truth. " Opinions," he had said, " are stronger than armies." [1]

The change, however, was not due to the Peace Society. It was due to the Eastern Question. Napoleon had lost his character as the great enemy of European Liberalism, not because of any change of heart in England, but because the Tsar had taken his place. A new actor was playing the rôle and there was no room for an understudy.

This reversal was not quite so sudden as it seemed. The first step had been taken unconsciously. In February, followers of Mazzini had made an attempt upon Milan and a would-be assassin, no doubt a follower of somebody, had tried to kill the Emperor of Austria. The Austrian Government had complained that England's habit of harbouring refugees had made these attempts possible, and a rumour had spread that the Government was to be requested to surrender Mazzini and Kossuth. A debate in Parliament proved that the rumour was unfounded, and Lord Lyndhurst's speech established England's legal right to give sanctuary to all the revolutionaries of Europe, if she wished. [2]

The importance of this incident lay in the fact that it recalled the events of 1849. [3] The Austrian Emperor, newspaper readers were reminded, had always been cruel and vindictive—this was but another proof of it. It was a good thing Lord Palmerston was still there to prevent the Government from faltering. He had been firm with

---

[1] *Herald of Peace*, April 1853.
[2] Vide Hansard, 5/3/53. For an inside account of the affair vide Henry Greville, ii. 40–5.
[3] Vide above, 50–1.

Austria and Russia in 1849 and he would be again.
On a matter like this, said *The Morning Post,*
no amicable arrangement could ever be made
with a tyranny such as Austria.[1]

The incident might have been forgotten had
it not been that it was immediately followed by
the announcement of Prince Menschikoff's demands
upon Turkey. So not only Austria but the Tsar
had recommenced his old aggressions ! And once
again it was Turkey upon which the attack was
being made ! Where was Lord Palmerston ?

This attitude was taken instinctively. The events
of 1849 were once more vividly before the minds
of newspaper readers. The complex problems which
perplexed the Cabinet did not disturb the ordinary
citizen. In his head was a picture of a past event ;
he thought he saw its repetition. On that occasion
England's destiny had been in the hands of his
favourite statesman. Our intervention, he believed,
had saved Turkey. Our action this time must
be equally prompt and vigorous.

What then was our action to be ? According
to his picture of 1849, the right method of procedure
when dealing with the Tsar was to dispatch a
fleet against him immediately. He read with
wonder that this was what Louis Napoleon was
doing and with shame that we were not acting
with him. His judgment of Napoleon had clearly
been mistaken : his worst fears of the Coalition
Cabinet were confirmed. What excuse had our
Government for its inaction ? What did *The
Times* say ? That Turkey was a decaying and
barbaric, as well as a pagan Empire ? This was
outrageous. If Turkey was weak then there was

---

[1] 10/3/53. *The Times,* 28/2/53, declared that since " we are a
nation of refugees," the Emperors had better put their own houses
in order or they might themselves be soon seeking an asylum with us.

all the more reason to aid her. Moreover, Palmerston himself had said that Turkey was reforming, and everyone knew that with Lord Stratford at the Porte, Turkey was becoming tolerant and would soon be converted. No, these were the merest excuses. There could be no two opinions about it. Our fleet had not accompanied Napoleon's because Aberdeen, who was notoriously a friend of the Tsar, was in Russian pay, and Palmerston, decoyed away to the Home Office, was gagged and helpless.

Now this series of mental events is not imaginary. Every newspaper writer, who had not direct inspiration from someone actually engaged in the negotiations, passed through some, if not every one, of these stages. It was a natural sequence of thought leading to an inevitable conclusion. There were two obstacles to overcome before the picture could be complete. The first was distrust of Napoleon. This proved easy to change into a compensating enthusiasm. The second—the evil record of Turkey—was a more difficult obstruction, and it was only after a prolonged struggle that zealously Protestant newspapers were able to put a note of confidence into their demand for a war on behalf of Islam.

There were, however, two papers which were, as we know, in constant communication with members of the Government—*The Times* with Clarendon, and *The Morning Post* with Palmerston. In both papers, therefore, we find a more complex view of the situation. *The Morning Post*, at the outset, found the question difficult, and began by complimenting the Tsar while expressing detestation of the policy of former Tsars. " Hitherto the Emperor Nicholas has displayed an appreciation so profound and so just of his duties and the rights of other Powers that it may be hoped that he will not now depart from this policy of good sense and moderation." [1] It was at first confident that the affair would soon be settled, and continued for some time to consider the Emperor of Austria more dangerous than the Tsar.[2] But after the first two months this disagreement with other papers ceased. It is true that the Government, which included Palmerston, was not openly attacked.[3] But Lord Palmerston, after all, though not unreservedly accepting the ignorant view of the outside world, agreed with the popular idea of what should be England's policy. It is not, therefore, in any way surprising to find that *The Morning Post* was soon a leader in the cry for strong measures against Russia. *The Morning Chronicle*, too, though beginning in the cautious manner befitting an organ of the Peelites, soon joined in the popular cry. The editor's sympathies were with Lord Palmerston.[4]

The Times, from the outset, adopted the attitude of Lord Aberdeen. On February 28th Delane had " a long chat with the Premier " and " found him very strong against the Turks." [5] *The Times*, therefore, continued to insist that Turkey was breaking up and that the Tsar was right in looking after the Christians in a decaying pagan Empire. We, too, should do well to consider beforehand the probable effects of its dissolution. For these distressed Christians it is deeply concerned : " We are bound by every consideration

[1] 21/3/53.

[2] E.g. 6/4/53. Vide below, 129.

[3] E.g. 4/6/53. *The Morning Post* stated in a somewhat marked way that matters could be safely left to a Cabinet which contained Clarendon, Lord John, and Palmerston.

[4] Vide above, 93.

[5] Reeve, i. 288.

of humanity, civilization, and justice to trust that it may be the will of Providence to restore these provinces and their miserable inhabitants to a purer faith and a milder sway." [1]

When, towards the end of March, Napoleon dispatched the French fleet to the Dardanelles, Henry Reeve " at once saw . . . that the French had got into a scrape in which we should not follow them." [2] He was right : the Cabinet refused to co-operate with Napoleon and the fleet was kept in home waters. During the next two days, therefore (March 21st and 22nd), in the leading articles in *The Times* Reeve declared that " it must be borne in mind that the prime aggressor of which Turkey has to complain is France " [3] that it was a " mockery to suppose that this country can be made a catspaw of the French Government," and that it was England's duty to abstain from any interference.[4] He heard from Delane that Aberdeen entirely concurred in this position. These articles, however, so annoyed the French that a few days later, Lord Clarendon " entreated " Reeve " not to fall upon them." He consequently wrote an article next day which he " afterwards heard had, oddly enough, delighted both Russia and France." [5] For the next two months, *The Times* kept strictly to this attitude : that there was no reason to think that the Tsar meant " to risk war upon such a question " and that England could only aid in the negotiations if she avoided hostile measures such as that taken by Napoleon.

[1] *Times*, 7/3/53.

[2] Reeve, i. 295 ; letter March 20th.

[3] There was something to be said for this view. The question of the Holy Places had been re-opened in the preceding year in order to please French Catholics.

[4] *Times*, March 21st and 22nd.

[5] Reeve, i. 295–6. Vide *Times*, 28/3/53.

Every other newspaper in the country took, as we have said, a different view of the situation. The occasion was seized as an opportunity for discrediting Aberdeen and destroying the great position of *The Times*. Facts had little to do with the formation of opinion.

Against the view that Turkey must soon break up the other papers protested; some of them with moderation at first and increasing violence; others with a violence at first which it was impossible afterwards to increase. Turkey, *The Morning Post* found to be, as Lord Palmerston said, a tolerant State, and although poorly governed at present, capable of improvement.[1] *The Manchester Guardian* at first agreed that Turkey was weak, but found this a reason not for deserting her, but for continuing our protection. And there was another reason: " Turkey is a source of supply for some of our most important imports." [2] *The Daily News* was especially interested in our valuable trade with the Porte : it declared that the Tsar's " scandalous desire to despoil Turkey " would " overhang the markets of Europe for some time to come." Further, Constantinople itself was perhaps in danger ; if Russia should " succeed in reaching the Bosphorous," " adieu to everything like freedom of faith, of speech, of printed thought, and of trade." [3]

The plea that the Balkan peoples, for whom we had fought against Turkey, would prefer the so-called Christian despotism of the Tsar to the generous and tolerant rule of the Sultan, was denounced as pro-Russian or Austrian propaganda. *The Morning Herald* dubbed *The Times*, " our Hebrao-Austro-Russian contemporary," *The Daily News* referred to the " Brunmow organ," while

[1] E.g. 31/5/53. [2] 5/3/53; also cp. 26/3/53, 8/6/53. [3] 20/6/53.

trust in him.[1] This attitude, however, did not last long. By June the French Emperor's firm policy was everywhere held up as a contrast to that of our Government. If our fleet accompanied Napoleon's, the Tsar would give way and war would become unnecessary.[2] " England and France are the two policemen of Europe," said *The Press*, " and they can always keep the peace." [3]

In June, as we have seen, the Cabinet gave way to this demand " as the least measure which will satisfy public opinion." But the Cabinet was chiefly concerned at this period in gaining Austrian and Prussian help in the negotiations. If the Four Powers were united, Clarendon believed that terms could be arranged. The important thing was to conciliate Austria and not to drive the Tsar into further follies. On June 4th, therefore, he wrote to Reeve explaining the situation and asking him to avoid giving the Tsar " any just cause of irritation." " A disbelief in war would be the best tone, founded not alone upon the declared intentions of the Emperor to uphold the Turkish Empire, but upon the pacific principles which he has adopted throughout his reign." The leading articles in *The Times*, therefore, followed this suggestion and, while warning the Tsar that we were not to be intimidated, declared that the British Government had been right in its moderation, since only the " joint action of Europe is the true sanction of Public Law and Peace." [4] Lord Clarendon wrote thanking Reeve for his " excellent article " and continued to supply him with information concerning the one thing which could bring a peaceful solution—the unity of the Four Powers. " *The* difficulty," he wrote,

---

[1] 3/4/53.   [2] E.g. *D.N.* 30/5/53.
[3] 28/5/53.   [4] 6/6/53.

" is finding a decent mode of backing out for the Emperor." [1]

Now to the Opposition papers the idea that Austria might be upon the side of the allies could not occur. Austria and Russia were one in villainy. *The Morning Post*, accepting Lord Palmerston's view, had always been persistent in abuse of Francis Joseph and, until the middle of May, showed no signs of change. Then appeared an article, no doubt inspired by Palmerston,[2] admitting that Austria, " in whose interests it was," would perhaps aid in coercing the Tsar.[3] But *The Morning Post* found it impossible seriously to entertain the probability of an Austrian alliance and confidently expected her treachery.[4] In July, on the basis of an unfounded rumour from his friends in Paris, Mr. Borthwick declared that she had invaded Bosnia.[5]

Other papers, not troubled by hints from Lord Palmerston, knew nothing of the desirability of the Austrian alliance. They assumed that Austria would help Russia, and the fact that, in this case, the allies could not reach Russian troops in the Principalities was not noticed. The diplomats indeed knew that Austria's policy was the crux of the problem ; to the public it seemed irrelevant.

---

[1] Reeve, i. 304–6. Letters from Clarendon to Reeve, June 16th and 29th, July 3rd and 5th.

[2] I have no direct evidence that Palmerston inspired this particular article though we know that he was in constant touch with *The Morning Post*. The internal evidence is good. Other papers could not even entertain the idea, and *The Morning Post*, which had led in anti-Austrian sentiment, changes with visible reluctance.

[3] 19/5/53.   [4] 7/7/53.

[5] 11/7/53. *The Times* was more cautious. Cp. Reeve, i. 307. " There was a report in Paris that Austria is preparing to occupy Bosnia and Servia, but I have no news of it." There never was any news of it.

the double influence which acts on the paper. . . . When the two articles appeared in *The Times* to which I particularly allude, Clarendon approved of the first, and found great fault with the other, while Aberdeen wrote to Delane and expressed his strong approbation of the second." [1] It was Delane's policy to support the Cabinet, but what if the Cabinet was divided against itself ?

During the first six months of 1853, a somewhat curious relationship had existed between Cabinet and Public.

In the Cabinet itself there had been a difference of opinion between Palmerston and Aberdeen, but a joint policy had been arranged without great difficulty. The Premier had acquiesced in the dispatch of Lord Stratford to the Porte and had consented, against his better judgment, to send a fleet to the Dardanelles. But every member of the Cabinet agreed that any action against Russia must be taken in company, not only with Napoleon, but also with Austria and, if possible, Prussia. The Tsar's demands were not totally unexpected or unwarranted : diplomacy should easily adjust a matter which was only made difficult by Prince Menschikoff's arrogant behaviour and dangerous by the Tsar's precipitate action in crossing the Pruth. The problem was to gain the help of Austria and to find a formula which would guarantee Turkish sovereignty and satisfy such of the Russian demands as were just.

This, however, was not the problem of which the public was thinking. The revival of the Russian peril of 1849 had driven out the popular fear of Napoleon III. The Tsar seemed again

---

[1] Grev., vii. 74, written July 12th. Greville apparently refers to the articles quoted above, 9/7/53.

attempting a policy of fraud to which the Premier was either blind or subservient. *The Times* was his accomplice. Turkey, the defendant of the refugees, was likely to be overwhelmed. Opinion was still divided as to the character of this calamity. Turkey, after all, was not a Christian country, and her record, except for one bright incident, nor reassuring. But there was a comfortable tendency to accept the view that she was rapidly reforming. At any rate her existence was essential to our prosperity. Austria, notoriously subservient to Russia, was certainly treacherous. Constantinople, too, might at any moment be seized and our Eastern trade, as well as our naval supremacy and national honour, destroyed. It was the duty of the public to insist on our fleet being sent to prevent the occurrence of this catastrophe.

The public insisted. Our fleet was sent. It was now clear that Lord Palmerston, whose views had been advocated by *The Morning Post* could force the Cabinet to adopt a sound policy if sufficient weight of public opinion supported him in his lonely position.

CHAPTER VI

THE VIENNA NOTE

1. The Cabinet.
(July–October)

IN telling the story of a committee one member of which became a party to decisions notoriously at variance with his principles, Mr. J. M. Keynes wrote : " The President would be manœuvred off his ground, would miss the moment for digging his toes in, and, before he knew where he had been got to, it was too late." Lord Aberdeen had begun a similar course of slipping and hesitating and slipping again. When, at the beginning of June, he had allowed the fleet to sail to the Dardanelles in order " to satisfy public opinion," he had missed the first opportunity to dig his toes in. That he was partly conscious of this his letters show. In the very act of committing himself on behalf of Turkey, he wrote protesting against the suggestion that he was not perfectly free : " The only hostile operation contemplated by the Cabinet has been the defence of Constantinople against a Russian attack. How far we may contract engagements with the Porte, in the event of actual war, and under what circumstances we should find ourselves justified in being finally committed against Russia, ought to be the subject of future deliberation. We are at present bound by no stipulations of

134

treaty in this respect, and are free to adopt such a course as may appear most consistent with our real interests and honour." [1]

But this freedom was only theoretical. By the end of September Lord Aberdeen had again been manœuvred off his ground, and the Cabinet had become "finally committed against Russia," whether they admitted it or not.

In July there seemed an excellent prospect of peace. Out of a number of Notes suggested, one had been agreed upon by the Four Powers now in Council at Vienna. It was thought to remedy Russia's grievances without endangering the sovereignty of the Sultan. The fact that it originated with the Powers at Vienna and not with Napoleon or Stratford seemed to make its acceptance by the Tsar probable, and Lord Clarendon had great hopes of an early termination of his difficulties. Lord Palmerston, too, was now quite in accord with the rest of the Cabinet, and complimented Clarendon upon his management of the negotiations. [2]

On August 5th news came that the Tsar had accepted the Vienna Note. Most of the Cabinet thought the whole question at an end, though Clarendon was still doubtful. The Tsar had promised acceptance ; but what if the Turks, to whom, perhaps regrettably, the Note had not been presented, should make difficulties ? Lord Stratford, too, might "raise obstacles instead of using all his influence to procure their agreement." Clarendon, therefore, did not consider the Government "out of the wood." [3]

[1] Stanmore, *Aberdeen*, 227.

[2] Grev., vii. 78 ; Maxwell, ii. 16. " I can assure you that it is a great comfort and satisfaction for me to know that the conduct of foreign relations is in such able hands as yours." Palmerston to Clarendon at the end of July.

[3] Grev., vii. 80.

But for the moment all seemed well. The
administration had successfully introduced a
measure for the reorganization of the Government
of India, and Mr. Gladstone had defended his
Budget in a speech of extraordinary ability.[1] If
the Cabinet could now announce an amicable
settlement between Turkey and Russia, their opponents, both in the House and in the Press, would
be routed at every point. " The Queen," wrote
Greville, is " very smiling " and the " Government
are in high spirits at the prospect of winding up
their prosperous session with the settlement of the
Eastern Question." [2]

This success, however, was denied them.
Clarendon's fears had been only too well founded.
The Turks only accepted the Note on condition that certain modifications were introduced.
Unable, therefore, to quiet their critics by a
simple announcement of a peaceful settlement,
the Government found it necessary to defend
their policy. Everything depended upon Lord
Palmerston. If his support of Clarendon's course
should be wholehearted, Tory and Cobdenite critics
would be alike ineffective.

In the early stages of the debate Clarendon and
Lord John were severely handled by Tory opponents,
and their replies were " tame, meagre, and un-
satisfactory." Then Cobden spoke. He declared
that the " independence of the Turkish Empire
was an empty phrase," and, perhaps a little
tactlessly, reminded the House that, unlike his
opponents, he had studied Turkish administration
on the spot and did not take facts on hearsay.
Neither did he confine himself to the Eastern
Question : he dealt also with war in general.
" The Government," he added, " have done wisely

[1] Morley, *Gladstone*, i. 469.   [2] Grev., vii. 80.

in not listening to the cry of the newspapers, some of which profess democratic principles, as if democracy ever gained anything by war."

Lord Palmerston was roused and the Government was safe. He " fell upon Cobden with great vigour and success." Cobden's facts failed to interest him. " I assert without fear of contradiction from anyone who knows anything about it," he said, " that so far from having gone back, Turkey has made greater progress and improvement than any other country in the same period." As for Cobden's trade statistics he brushed them aside. Why did England go to war in the past ? " Why, sir, we went to war for the liberties of Europe and not for the purpose of gaining so much per cent on our exports." Criticism was over. Like newspaper editors, members of Parliament approved if Palmerston was satisfied. Mr. Danby Seymour expressed the prevailing sentiment when he declared that : " He was glad that the Ministry contained a nobleman of proper English spirit, who, he was certain, would not consent to remain a member of any administration unless a policy were followed conducive to the honour of the country." [1]

Parliament was adjourned and the Government had only the newspapers to face. " We shall now be able," wrote Sir James Graham, " to act without interrogatories administered in Parliament and without speeches calculated to mislead the Turk into false confidence that he will be supported in resistance to reasonable demands. This delusion may lead him into a pitfall." Clarendon agreed that " the Turks seem to be

[1] Hansard, cxxxix. 1622, 1798–1810 ; Grev., vii. 80–1. Cp. his description of the effect of Palmerston's speech with that given by Mr. Layard, ii. 247.

getting more stupid and obstinate every day,"
and that the difficulty now lay in getting them
to agree to any terms which the Tsar could be
expected to accept.[1]

For Turkey had now become the great obstacle
to peace : the Tsar was merely looking for " some
mode of backing down." News of the warlike
spirit at Constantinople continually arrived. " The
conduct of the Porte," wrote Aberdeen," is suicidal.
It can only be explained by a desire that the affair
shall end in war." [2] Lord Clarendon agreed with
him and believed that Lord Stratford was encouraging the warlike spirit at the Porte.

" I have all along felt that Stratford would
allow no plan of settlement to succeed which did
not originate with himself," wrote Clarendon to
Lord John, and Lord Cowley who had received
an account from De la Cour at Constantinople
fully confirmed his impression.[3] " Publicly, and
officially, Lord Stratford has obeyed instructions
and called upon the Ottoman Government to
accept the Vienna Note ; but he lets it be seen
that his private opinion is at variance with his
official language. De la Cour asserts further that
to his *intimes*, Lord Stratford uses the most violent
language, that he disapproves all the proceedings
at Vienna, declares that war was preferable to
such a conclusion. Then he goes on to say that
they shall know his name is Canning, that he will
resign, that he knows that the Government is
not united on this question, and that a change
must take place there which will bring into power

[1] Maxwell, ii. 17.
[2] Ibid., 19–20.
[3] Ibid., 18. De la Cour was French Ambassador at the Porte.
Westmorland, at Vienna, reported to the same effect. Grev., vii. 86.
Meyendorff, also at Vienna, wrote to Aberdeen with a similar
account, 16/9/53.

the friends and supporters of his policy in Turkey."
Sir James Graham was equally sure that Stratford
was the obstacle. On September 3rd he wrote
that Europe must not " be involved in war because
Canning is resolved to embroil matters at home
and abroad in the hope of attaining a triumph
for his own morbid vanity and implacable anti-
pathies."

If these were the opinions expressed by Cabinet
Ministers, why was not Lord Stratford recalled ?
It was the critical moment for Aberdeen. Now
or never must he dig his toes in. But to recall
Stratford was no easy matter. Lord Cowley had
reported that Stratford had threatened to resign
and destroy the Government. If so, it was no
idle boast. His hold on the Press, the natural
popularity of his strong anti-Russian policy, and,
above all, his friendship with Lord Palmerston,
would have made his recall or resignation fatal
to the Ministry. Nevertheless, Aberdeen seems
to have made up his mind and, on August 20th,
actually wrote to the Queen to prepare her for
Stratford's resignation. Sir James Graham was
in hearty agreement. " You should be ready
to supersede him without the loss of a day," he
wrote, " and to send either Bulwer or Howden,
to give effect on the spot to the fixed purpose of
the allies." [1] Clarendon, however, though admitting

---

[1] The question of Stratford's recall arose again in November.
The Queen suggested it and Aberdeen replied that: " He could
not answer for the effect it might produce in the country, and in
the Government." *Correspondence*, 28/11/53. It is worth while to
note the attitude of our other ambassadors. Sir G. Seymour at
St. Petersburg had ceased to anticipate a peaceful settlement with
pleasure. On August 18th he wrote : " The Russians are great
rogues and the Emperor worthy of being at the head of such a
people. . . . *I am ashamed to say that it will be almost painful to
me if the thing is patched up without the Russian having been taught*

that Stratford was "very warlike, and rejoiced in the state of preparedness in which the Porte has put itself" [1] said that "there was no official evidence that he had failed in doing his duty fairly by his own Government : therefore it would be out of the question to recall him." [2] "He has never," he wrote, "entered sincerely into the views of the Government, and has been making political capital for himself. However, there he is and we must make the best of him."

While Aberdeen was hesitating an event occurred which rendered it impossible to recall Stratford or to insist upon the Turks accepting the Vienna Note. A dispatch from Nesselrode appeared in a Berlin paper which made it clear that the interpretation placed upon the modified clauses by Russia was not that originally intended by the allies. The Press, which had lately become more reconciled to a diplomatic settlement, burst forth again into furious wrath with Russia. [3] The effect on Palmerston and Russell seems to have been similar. Palmerston took no trouble to conceal his belief that the existence of the Government depended on him and showed that he would be no party to coercing Turkey. He was apt to speak of war with Russia in a nonchalant, jaunty manner which terrified some of his colleagues. [4]

Lord John was disappointed at not taking Aber-

---

that Cronstadt and Sevastopol never were dropped in the Styx, whatever the rest of the Empire may have been. They sadly want a lesson and I should have been glad if they had got it before their fleet is better manned." Parker, ii. 223. As for Westmorland at Vienna, Clarendon suggested to Aberdeen on October 10th that they should "send someone as coadjutor to our faithful but feeble Westmorland."

[1] Reeve, i. 309.   [2] Grev., vii. 88–90.
[3] Vide below, 150–2.   [4] Grev., vii. 91.

deen's place at the head of affairs, and had become somewhat restive and unreliable.[1] At first he had seemed to agree with Aberdeen that the acceptance of the Note should be the condition of our help to Turkey.[2] Immediately afterwards he wrote to the contrary effect. On several occasions he threatened to break up the Ministry by resigning.[3] On September 17th he wrote to Clarendon warning him that if pressure was put upon the Turks he should probably " decline any responsibility for it." On the 27th he became more emphatic. " As to the question of war for us, I had already considered all the evils you mention, and they are only to be encountered *if our honour is at stake*. I know something of the English people, and feel sure that they would fight to the stumps for the honour of England. To have held out such encouragement to the Turks as we have done and afterwards to desert them, would be felt as deep disgrace and humiliation by the whole country."[4]

Other members of the Cabinet agreed that

[1] Aberdeen had told Russell that he would resign in his favour at the first opportunity. The opportunity did not arrive, not because of unwillingness on Aberdeen's part, but because Russell could not have formed a Cabinet. Sir J. Graham at Balmoral wrote to Aberdeen : " The Queen intimated to me that if Peel's friends remained united Lord John must see the impossibility of power passing into the hands of an exclusive Whig Party. ' The silent members of the Cabinet ' have hitherto been with you. . . . The reunion of Lord John and Palmerston is certainly formidable, but much will depend on the Righteousness of the Cause, and on the Purity of Motives and Conduct."

[2] Letter to Aberdeen. *Correspondence*, 27/8/53.

[3] Grev., vii. 97–9; Maxwell, ii. 21–3; Argyll, i. 463. In view of these accounts it is impossible to accept Spencer Walpole's account of Lord John's conduct at this time.

[4] Cp. this with Lord John's assertion (Russell, 271), that he would have "insisted on making Turkey accept the Vienna Note if he had been Prime Minister." Also vide Stanmore, *Aberdeen*, 228 ; *Letters*, ii. 557–8.

Nesselrode's dispatch had killed the Vienna Note. Lord Clarendon wrote : " We cannot press the Turks too hard about the Note because public opinion would be against it, and secondly, because they would fight it out single-handed." [1] Prince Albert and the Queen, who had been in favour of peremptory dealing with the Porte, now felt that a new start must be made.[2] The view of the peace party in the Cabinet was summed up by Sidney Herbert when he wrote that " the Note had now been so blown upon and each party so committed against it, that it is hopeless to press it further." [3]

The Vienna Note was abandoned. At the same time a further step was taken which made future negotiations more difficult. In Constantinople enthusiasm for war had led to riots in which " the lives and property of British subjects were in danger." Moreover, storms in Besika Bay made it necessary to remove the fleet to some other harbour, and the state of public opinion made its withdrawal impossible. On September 23rd, a dispatch was sent to Stratford ordering him to summon the fleet to the Bosphorus in defiance of the treaty of 1841, which closed the Straits to all ships of war except those of Turkey. Less than a fortnight before, Aberdeen had written to the Queen : " It would be an act of gross inconsistency to enter the Dardanelles and to violate a treaty at the very moment that Russia had complied with the demands made by the Four Powers who were parties to that engagement." [4] Yet

[1] Maxwell, ii. 20.
[2] *Letters*, ii. 550. Albert had changed his mind about the Tsar's intentions. A month before he had written to Aberdeen that he almost felt " tempted to abandon the Turks to their fate." *Correspondence*, 25/8/53.
[3] Stanmore, *Sidney Herbert*, i. 207.
[4] *Correspondence*, Aberdeen to the Queen, 12/9/53.

the advance was made. It roused bitter hostility in Russia and irretrievably committed England to Turkey's support.[1]

Lord Aberdeen had again given way, and, as usual, *The Press* was careful to call attention to his surrender. A revised verse from Thomas Hood served as an " epitaph " for the week.

> Speak of him tenderly,
> Gently and humanly,
> All that is left of him
> Now is pure womanly.[2]

2. The Public.

(July–October)

During July and August the attack on the Government and abuse of *The Times* never ceased.

[1] Cp. *E.P.*, ii. 126–7 for Count Nesselrode's protest and Clarendon's reply.

[2] 10/9/53. "Epitaph on Lord Aberdeen from Hood's ' Bridge of Sighs.' " On the same date appears the following :—

"A CARD PARTY AT THE FOREIGN OFFICE.

ABERDEEN : ' Shuffle, Clarendon.'

CLARENDON : ' You are always making me shuffle. It's Palmerston's lead.'

PALMERSTON : ' I wish it was.'

LORD JOHN RUSSELL : ' I've followed your lead, Palmerston.'

PALMERSTON : ' And won the trick. It's a way people have who do as I bid them. If somebody I know had trumped Menshikoff's ultimatum with Dundas's Broadside, as I advised, we four should not be sitting in a back office in the first week of September instead of shooting partridges. However, we won't talk of that, or the Premier will go revoking to the damage of Clarendon's peace of mind.'

ABERDEEN : ' I wish ye'd just play. Dinna talk so much.'

PALMERSTON : ' You never see me put out.'

ABERDEEN (spitefully) : ' Not since Christmas twelvemonth.'

PALMERSTON (laughing) : ' Very good, very good indeed. Who says the old gentleman's memory is failing ? Christmas had a February after it, hadn't it, Russell ? '

RUSSELL : ' Never mind. You played the deuce ? '

PALMERSTON : ' I did, though I ought not to say so.' "

But there were considerable fluctuations of opinion as to the necessity of war. At the beginning of July the news that Russian troops had crossed the Pruth had, as we have seen, produced a sentiment in favour of immediate hostilities, except in those papers which received Government inspiration. Even *The Times* had become doubtful. But when it was realized that our fleet had at length moved out to join the French one, and that a Note had been sent to Russia, there was again a tendency to expect the Tsar to give way.

At the beginning of August came another fluctuation. The Government, when asked for information in the Commons, seemed unwilling to give it, and an unlucky speech by Clarendon in the House of Lords suggested that war was probable. For a few days there was " a great fall of funds and the depreciation of every sort of security." " Everybody," wrote Greville, " became persuaded that war was inevitable."[1]

Into the midst of this panic came the announcement that the Tsar had accepted the Vienna Note. It was now impossible to continue a belief in war. Russia apparently had given way. We had successfully repeated 1849. *The Times* erroneously considered the matter at an end and even reported that : " The Sultan has gratefully acceded to the terms recommended by the Conference of Vienna and it is understood that the Principalities will speedily be evacuated." [2] *The Morning Post* announced that " the Eastern Question is settled," and *The Morning Chronicle* concurred.[3] *The Manchester Guardian* found the settlement a triumph for principle of joint action by the Powers. Turkey, of course, would assent

---

[1] Grev., vii. 79.   [2] 15/8/53.   [3] 11/8/53.

at once to terms arranged for her by the allies.[1]
The Herald of Peace was jubilant. " We presume,"
it wrote, " that we may now say that all danger
of a war in the East is at an end." [2]   Other papers
were less easy to satisfy. They had been sure
that the Tsar would not accept. It was difficult
to feel elated that the war, so confidently anticipated, would not after all occur.   Some editors
thought that there could be only one explanation
of Russia's willingness—our Government, known
to be Russian in sympathy, had offered the Tsar
terms which humiliated Turkey. What were the
terms ? No one knew exactly, but a question
by Clanricarde in the House of Lords on August
12th provided the clue.   The terms did not
include a demand for immediate evacuation of
the Principalities.[3]   Clarendon was apparently
trusting in the " good faith of the Tsar " to
evacuate after the conclusion of preliminary
terms. Was there ever clearer proof of Russian
intrigue in a Cabinet ? The fact that such a
demand would necessarily have meant war was
realized by diplomats but not by newspaper
editors.

The Daily News, therefore, denounced the terms ;
they were merely offered in order to give Russia
time to complete the careful duplicity which
had characterized her policy for centuries. The
Spithead naval review, intended by the Government to reassure the public, was, *The Daily News*
declared, but a method of diverting the public
from insisting that the Navy be put to its proper

[1] 10/8/53.
[2] September Number.
[3] Hansard, cxxix. 1425. Clarendon agreed that the evacuation of
the Principalities was " a *sine qua non* of any agreement whatever,"
but admitted that evacuation was expected to follow, not precede a
settlement.

" that is not a match for Russia in strength when she is the aggressor : but there is not one that is a match for her in intelligence."

Turkey, then, was stronger than Russia, and all the negotiations were fraudulent. Conferences were merely Russian contrivances to gain the aid of English and French politicians in destroying Turkey. If left alone, Turkey would easily turn Gortschakoff out of the Principalities and the Tsar would return to the Kremlin to wait for the next opportunity of descending upon the free subjects of the Sultan. *The Times,* he said, continually repeated a " liturgy " ; " the Christian subjects of the Porte require and deserve pro- tection . . . and his (the Tsar's) four Archangels in Downing Street respond Amen ! " In fact the diplomatic conflict was only a semblance— a collusive action in which England was prosecuting Russia by arrangement, so that Turkey might be despoiled with all the forms of legality.[1]

During August and September, however, Mr. Urquhart's was a lonely voice. No one else believed in Lord Palmerston's guilt and few thought it possible that our aid to Turkey was really a method of helping the Tsar. Moreover, with the adjournment of Parliament in the middle of August interest in the Eastern Question grew less. Most papers believed that the matter would now be peacefully settled. The bright hope of a glorious war was tarnished by the dust of diplomacy.

At the beginning of August came the news that Turkey wished for modifications in the Vienna Note, a fortnight later that the Tsar had refused to accept them.

---

[1] Urquhart, in *The Morning Advertiser,* 10/8/53–20/9/53. Only slightly less violent was Walter Savage Landor. See his letters in *The Examiner,* July 1853–March 1855.

The Morning Post was frankly tired of the subject. Russia, by her original acceptance of the Note, had shown that she would give way; with Lord Palmerston in the Cabinet the terms arranged would be honourable, and modifications and counter-proposals were in the nature of diplomacy.[1] *The Globe* declared that both Russia and Turkey had the right to modify the terms and saw no reason why peace should not be made.[2] *The Morning Herald* wavered for a moment, but decided that since the Tsar had shown signs of surrender, our united demand might induce him to withdraw from the Principalities without actual hostilities.[3]

The Times went further than this. Delane knew that the Cabinet now found Turkey less tractable than Russia. He agreed with Aberdeen in wishing to force Turkey to accept the Vienna Note. But the dispatches he received from Constantinople were becoming increasingly difficult to use as the basis of pacific " leaders." He therefore wrote to his Eastern Correspondent informing him that it would be impossible to retain his services if he persisted in taking a line so diametrically opposed to the interests of this country. " You seem to imagine," he went on, " that England can desire nothing better than to sacrifice all its greatest interests and its most cherished objects to support barbarism against civilization, the Moslem against the Christian, slavery against liberty, to exchange peace for war—all to oblige the Turk . . . when no amount of protection can preserve his boasted ' independence and integrity.' . . . I trust, therefore, that in future you will have the modesty to forbear from offhand censures of English policy, to devote your whole attention to collecting

[1] September 5th–12th.   [2] 15/9/53.   [3] 15/9/53.

disaster.[1] *The Daily News* felt that England's honour was at stake, and asked if Aberdeen was merely stupid or whether he was a " willing dupe." " Why," it demanded, " was the fleet to pass the Dardanelles ? If the Cabinet hoped in this way to lull public opinion into a false security it miscalculated. The fleets were only going up to Constantinople in order to " force Turkey to humiliate herself ! "[2] The public, if not the Government, must rally to the aid of the Porte. For the first time there was complete unity in the Press. Even *The Times* admitted that Turkey had, after all, been justified in rejecting the Note. Delane, however, betrayed the influence of Clarendon when he added that action against Russia must be taken only by the Four Powers, and regretted that Austria showed signs of retreating.[3] In this *The Times* stood alone. With other newspapers the associations of years of antipathy to Austria still remained. It was believed that if Austria entered the lists at all, it would be in behalf of Russia.[4]

[1] 28/9/53.
[2] *D.N.*, 26/9/53. This remark is almost certainly an example of Urquhart's influence. From where else could the idea have come ?
[3] September 22nd–24th.
[4] An incident which occurred at the end of September, though not in itself connected either with Austria or the Eastern Question, revised the dislike of Austria and demonstrated the popular belief in her complicity in the tyranny of the Tsar. On September 25th it was announced that a certain Miss Cunningham had been arrested in Tuscany for distributing Protestant literature. The story recalled Gladstone's exposure of Neapolitan prisons and treatment of rebels by Austrian generals in 1849. Many newspapers were, therefore, extremely indignant with " Papal and Austrian tyranny." Cp. *Morning Post, Times, Globe* and *Daily News*, September 26th to 28th. *The Daily News*, 26th, in an " imaginary conversation," shows a recollection of Palmerston's *civis Romanus sum* speech, comparing Miss Cunningham to St. Paul pleading Roman citizenship. *The Morning Chronicle* took an unusual and lofty view of the situation, 27/9/53. It wrote : " It would have exceeded the ingenuity of anyone but a Tuscan official to commit such a combination

It was no longer only in the newspapers that Austria and Russia were denounced. For the first time large and enthusiastic public meetings were called upon the Eastern Question. That the Vienna Note should be withdrawn, that Turkey, which was everywhere loudly cheered, should be aided, not merely by the presence of our fleet, but by its active participation against Russia, that our full support should be given to Louis Napoleon, whose name was now received with enthusiasm ; these were resolutions passed in many parts of the country and reported in full in the daily papers.[1] It was in view of this unanimity of public sentiment that the Cabinet reluctantly abandoned the Vienna Note instead of attempting to use it as a basis for further negotiation.

At the beginning of October, therefore, the negotiations stood exactly where they had in June. The problem was still to find a formula. There was no new point in dispute, no alteration in the demands of either party. The Tsar, the Austrian Government, and the English Cabinet were all still sincerely anxious for peace. But though the diplomatic situation was unchanged, the difficulty of obtaining peace was immensely enhanced.

---

of unprofitable outrages on our most cherished prejudices. To imprison a British subject, and that British subject a lady, and that lady one of the preferred race of Scots, and that Scotch gentlewoman a true blue Presbyterian . . . a lineal descendant of John Knox in a Tuscan *ergastulo causa religionis*. . . . To complete her religious martyrdom Miss Cunningham is in prison for circulating *The Pilgrim's Progress* ! A young Scottish lady of gentle birth, a Presbyterian, a descendant of John Knox in an Italian dungeon, damp and dirty, and living on mouldy bread and putrid water—all for the sake of Bunyan's immortal and, to our minds, most tedious allegory." "But Hood," *The Morning Chronicle* added, " was right when he said:—

> ! People who hold such absolute opinions,
> Should stay at home in Protestant dominions.' "

[1] Vide below, 183 *seq.*

on pain of a declaration of war. Clarendon, who had written to Stratford asking him to exert his influence to prevent the Sultan precipitating hostilities,[1] heard of Turkey's action with the utmost disgust. The news arrived on October 5th and he immediately wrote to Sidney Herbert pointing out that the peaceful overture of the Tsar must now necessarily be disregarded. " Things get worse and worse," he wrote. " The beastly Turks have actually declared war : so there is an end of the Olmütz arrangement, out of which something might possibly have been made; but it's all over now; " and Sidney Herbert replied : " That the Turkish declaration of war greatly aggravates our difficulties, no one can deny. It does not destroy the possibility but it greatly lessens the probability of peace." [2]

On October 5th, Clarendon wrote again summing up the situation. As usual the real difficulty was public opinion.

" The public seems to think that there is nothing to do but to declare war against Russia, just when she is yielding the point in dispute, and back the Turk, just when he acts contrary to our advice ; and thus, without any guarantee on our part obliging us so to act, and without any English or European interest at stake, if the question of the Note be adjusted, as I think it would be, or rather would

---

[1] Stratford had formally protested against the declaration of war, but had refused to exert his personal influence to prevent a step of which he undoubtedly approved. Cp. his letter explaining his conduct to Clarendon, 17/10/53 ; Stanmore, *Sidney Herbert*, i. 196–7, where his conduct at this time is discussed. Clarendon wrote, 11/9/53 : " It is quite clear that the Turks don't want a settlement. The titular Sultan is for peace, but the real Sultan (Stratford) thinks that now or never is the time for putting an end to Russia. I am afraid there is trouble in store for us."

[2] Maxwell, ii. 30.

have been if the Turks could have been kept quiet.
I believe they expect to take Petersburg before
Christmas ! " [1]

On October 7th, the Cabinet reassembled after
an interval of six weeks. Lord Palmerston wished
to support the Turkish declaration of war by
sending the fleet into the Black Sea and suggested
that the Russian admiral at Sevastopol should be
informed that " any Russian ship-of-war found
cruising in the Black Sea would be detained and
be given over to the Turkish Government." [2]
Clarendon moved and carried a more moderate
proposal. Stratford was ordered to summon the
fleets into the Black Sea for " strictly defensive "
purposes in the event of an actual declaration of
war by Turkey.[3]

Of this meeting of the Cabinet Aberdeen wrote
that the " aspect of the Cabinet was, on the whole,
very good. Gladstone active and energetic for
peace : Argyll, Herbert, Charles Wood, and Granville all in the same sense. Newcastle not quite
so much so : Lansdowne not so warlike as formerly ; Palmerston urged his views perseveringly
but not disagreeably. The Chancellor said little,
but was evidently peaceful. Molesworth was not
present, some mistake having been made in sending
him notice." [4]

The Cabinet, then, was not as yet divided
into parties, and on the 9th the Cabinet meeting, said Clarendon, was " almost harmonious ; "

---

[1] Stanmore, *Sidney Herbert*, i. 203.
[2] Memorandum to Aberdeen before the Cabinet meeting, October
7th. Ashley, ii. 41.
[3] Aberdeen again agreed to this with some reluctance. In a letter
to Sir J. Graham next day (October 8th) he explained that since
no attack on Turkish territory was likely to be made by the Tsar,
our fleet would not be involved.
[4] *Correspondence*, 8/10/53. Aberdeen to Sir James Graham.

Palmerston being "less cocky," and Aberdeen "less timid."

This harmony, however, became increasingly difficult to maintain. Lord Palmerston was convinced that England must necessarily be involved in the Turkish war with Russia. " We passed the Rubicon," he wrote a little later, " when we first took part with Turkey and sent our squadrons to her support." [1] Lord Lansdowne, the Duke of Newcastle, and Sir William Molesworth, though less convinced of the necessity of war, were substantially in agreement. Lord John was still in a difficult mood. He now urged that Parliament should be summoned early in November. To the Peelites this seemed a declaration of open warfare. A majority of the Commons would support the Whig leaders : it would certainly demand hostilities with Russia and negotiations would be at an end. Speaking of this proposal, Sir James Graham wrote to Aberdeen : " The trenches are opened and you must be on your guard ! This from the Leader of the House is a formidable move." [2] Parliament, however, was not summoned and on October 14th the Cabinet again dispersed for a fortnight. Discussion continued by letter, and those members of the Cabinet who were in London met with frequency.

There was now under consideration a Note drafted by Lord Stratford. Among other points in its favour it was believed that Lord Stratford would hardly recommend the Porte to refuse his own suggestions. Lord Aberdeen, who regretted that the Olmütz overture had been neglected, was now determined that this new proposal should lay down our final terms and that we should inform Turkey that their refusal would mean the end of

[1] Ashley, ii. 45.   [2] *Correspondence*, 13/10/53.

our support. Believing that the terms offered all that Turkey could justly require, he urged that Turkey should be informed that :—

" The Four Powers would not permit themselves, in consequence of unfounded objections, or by the declaration of war, which they have already condemned, to be drawn into a policy inconsistent with the peace of Europe, as well as with the true interests of Turkey itself."

This proposal he made to all the important members of the Cabinet. He wrote to Mr. Gladstone :—

" I believe we are now arrived at the last step it may be possible for us to take. . . . The Turks, with all their barbarism, are cunning enough, and see clearly the advantages of their situation. Step by step they have drawn us into a position in which we are more or less committed to their support. . . . I have thought it necessary to propose such an addition to the declaration of the Four Powers as is contained in the enclosed paper. It seems to me perfectly reasonable and just, considering our relations to the State on whose behalf we are attempting to mediate, and as offering the only chance of inducing the Turks to listen to pacific advice. . . . My own opinion is that it can only be objected to by those who really wish to make peace impossible." [1]

It seemed that Lord Aberdeen had found the place to dig his toes in. Mr. Gladstone in reply agreed that some such final statement of the limit of our aid was " indispensable." Two days later, however, he received a letter from the Prime Minister stating that he had decided not to press the clause which had been pronounced " indispensable." " I found," Aberdeen wrote, " both Palmer-

[1] Stanmore, *Aberdeen*, 232–4.

ston and Lord John were determined to resist it
to the utmost extremity, and I had to consider how
far I should be justified in creating a breach on
such a ground." [1] In the place of this clause he
persuaded his colleagues to demand from the Turks
a suspension of hostilities during the negotiation.
Owing to the insistence of Lord John, the demand,
as finally sent to the Turk, requested that this
suspension should last for a " reasonable time." [2]
The addition was not unimportant : a " reasonable time " in Turkey proved to be less than a
fortnight.

Lord Stratford's Note, therefore, was accepted
by the Sultan and sent to the Tsar, but its arrival
coincided with the news that Turkish troops had
opened hostilities. A month earlier Nicholas would
perhaps have accepted the terms offered him, but
now he was surrounded by a military party led by
religious enthusiasts, and his own pride was stung
by the first report of Turkish victories. The mood
of Olmütz had passed.[3]

Lord Aberdeen had missed the last opportunity
for retaining his freedom. He had given way once
more to public opinion. For to insist meant to
break up the Government ; to break up the Government meant that a war ministry would be formed.
Aberdeen, it is clear, would willingly have resigned,
but he believed that the new negotiations, now
reopened at Vienna, might succeed and that it was
his duty to fight for peace until the last. And if
Palmerston and Lord John resigned, how could
Aberdeen and his friends explain to an irate public,
now passionately in favour of Turkey, that it was

[1] *Correspondence*, October 18th–20th.
[2] *E.P.*, ii. 24/10/53 ; *Correspondence*, Lord John to Clarendon,
22/10/53.
[3] Cp. the account by August Loftus. Loftus, 1. 172.

necessary to force the Porte to adopt our Note without the opportunity of making alterations ? " To those," wrote Aberdeen, " who did not know all that had passed, such a condition would have appeared harsh and unjust, and I feel that it could not properly be made the ground of an irreconcilable difference in the Cabinet." [1]

2. " Odd Tempers and Queer Ways."

Lord Aberdeen had again given way, but his concession did not produce peace in his Cabinet. An interchange of memoranda between Prince Albert, Palmerston, and the Premier only emphasized the difference between the two latter. Palmerston insisted that England was now definitely committed to defend Turkey : " We must help Turkey out of her difficulties by negotiation, if possible, and if negotiation fails we must, by force of arms, carry her safely through her dangers." Aberdeen insisted that the Cabinet was " perfectly free to act as it thought best." Lord Clarendon became increasingly convinced that here Lord Palmerston was right and, differing from his Premier almost for the first time, wrote :—

" I must say that Palmerston makes out a very good case in support of his views and will be entitled to ask how far you consider we are bound by our recent acts, and at what point you will stop or recede. . . . We are now in an anomalous and painful position and, although I shall admit it to no one but yourself, I have arrived at the conviction that it might have been avoided by firmer language and a more decided course five months ago." [2]

[1] Stanmore, *Aberdeen*, 233.
[2] *Correspondence*, early in November.

Thus Cabinet meetings became increasingly difficult. Clarendon still found himself in an intermediate position between the placid militarism of Palmerston and the aggressive pacifism of Aberdeen. Palmerston, too, would throw out puzzling suggestions :—

"We should find it very useful," he wrote to Aberdeen on November 2nd, "to maintain in our communications with Brunmow a mysterious indefiniteness and uncertainty as to the manner and degree of assistance which England and France may deem it right to give to Turkey." [1]

Clearly he was becoming less and less interested in his duties as Home Secretary and his ambition to be conducting foreign affairs was less disguised. When asked by the Queen whether he had news about the strikes which were agitating the north of England he is reported to have answered absently : "No, Madam, I have heard nothing ; but it seems certain that the Turks have crossed the Danube." [2]

A new difficulty now arose. Lord John had pledged himself to bring in a Reform Bill and, in spite of difficulties in the Cabinet, felt his honour necessitated its early introduction. Lord Palmerston objected to its provisions ; Lord Lansdowne also seemed doubtful. The Eastern Question and the Reform Question became, as it were, alternate discords playing side by side in every Cabinet Council.

Perhaps the most unusual feature of the situation was that, whereas Lord John and Lord Palmerston separately seemed to hold much the same views on either subject, together they never agreed. "Palmerston and Lord John Russell are somewhat jealous of each other," wrote Sir James Graham

[1] *Correspondence*, 2/10/53. [2] Grev., vii. 107.

to Sidney Herbert, " and when one makes a concession, the other is disposed to hang back." [1]
In the same way, he might have added, if one makes
a new proposal the other attempts to rival it with
one still more popular. " John Russell," wrote
Greville after a conversation with Clarendon, " is
very reasonable, and agrees almost entirely with
Clarendon, but whenever he thinks he is going to
be outbid by Palmerston he is disposed to urge
some violent measures also." [2]

The Cabinet, moreover, was very sensitive to
outside opinion. Palmerston each day read *The
Times* and there found the views of Lord Clarendon.
Clarendon and Aberdeen had only to read *The
Morning Post* to find the views of Lord Palmerston.
The Cabinet, too, the Duke of Argyll tells us,
" was rather leaky. Things got out, we did not
quite know how, and reports, not very correct,
were circulated as to the part taken by individual
members." Argyll suggests that Sir William
Molesworth's habit of jotting things down in a
pocket-book may have been responsible for this
leakage. Through him things may have " reached
the ears of Villiers, Kinglake, and Hayward." [3]
The truth of Sir James Graham's remark at the
opening of the session became daily more obvious.
" There are," he had said of the new Cabinet,
" some odd tempers and queer ways among them." [4]
The odd tempers were increasingly odd and the
queer ways jarred no less from daily repetition.

[1] *Correspondence*, 22/10/53.
[2] Grev., vii. 108–9. Vide also below, 173, where Aberdeen says
Palmerston's resignation would " improve Lord John's foreign
policy."
[3] Argyll, i. 460.
[4] At one time an additional difficulty was Clarendon's conviction
that Palmerston was in secret communication with Stratford. Cp.
Lane Poole, ii. 231–2 ; Maxwell, ii. 28.

Lord Aberdeen was not the best of mediators. He felt the strain of disunity and was conscious that his position was a false one. The Duke of Argyll comments on the attitude of mind revealed in a letter written to him by the Premier on November 3rd :—

" It was an attitude of intense annoyance with some of the most insuperable facts of the position in which we and all our allies were placed. We were driving straight into a war for, and with, a barbarous Government which had declined to follow our advice, which, nevertheless, could not stand alone, a Government whose interests were only partially, and perhaps only very temporarily, coincident with our own. A change of circumstances, which was not at all unlikely to occur, might destroy even this partial coincidence in a moment. One of the most important of our allies, Austria, whose direct interests were very much more nearly concerned than ours, was at that very moment holding aloof and even threatening separation from us until she saw what our next move would be. I quite agreed with Aberdeen that the situation was intolerably provoking."

The Cabinet now presented a curious picture. One day Lord John Russell introduced a discussion of his Reform Bill; Lord Palmerston made a few minor criticisms. On reaching home, however, he wrote a letter to Lord John " denouncing the measure as unnecessary and unwise." Then, after criticizing the Bill in detail, he finally declared that he would consent to it. But having made a concession on one question, he felt entitled to have his own way on the other, and again urged the occupation of the Black Sea and the exclusion of the Russian fleet. Lord Aberdeen answered that this was equivalent to war, and

Lord Clarendon pointed out that the Four Powers at Vienna were at that moment engaged in arranging terms which might quite easily lead to peace. Hoping for the best, Clarendon would then write dispatches in a moderate tone which Lord Aberdeen would criticize as too warlike. On one occasion, when Aberdeen began to make objections, even Clarendon lost his temper and " broke out with the greatest vivacity." " Really this is too bad. You come now, after it has all been settled in the Cabinet, where you let it pass, and make all sorts of objections. And this is the way you do about everything ; you object to all that is proposed, and you never suggest anything yourself. What is it you want ? Will you say what you would have done ? " Aberdeen had nothing to say and knocked under. It was, indeed, as Clarendon said, a " regular scene." [1]

The crisis came early in December. Lord Palmerston continued to raise difficulties over the Reform Bill and constantly urged that the English fleet should occupy the Black Sea. At length, after some correspondence with the Queen and with other members of the Cabinet, Lord Aberdeen answered that he could see no way to meet him on either question. Lord Palmerston then wrote definitely stating that he found himself unable to concur in Lord John's Reform Bill, which he had warned Lord Aberdeen might be the case when the Ministry was formed. He added that he was not prepared at *his time of life* to encounter endless debates in the House of Commons on such a measure.[2] It so happened that the announcement of his resignation coincided with the detailed news of a Turkish

[1] Grev., vii. 109 ; Maxwell, ii. 27.
[2] Grev., vii. 113. " The first time," Clarendon said, " he had ever heard him acknowledge that he had a *time of life.*"

disaster in the Black Sea. A Russian fleet had caught six Turkish vessels cruising outside the open harbour of Sinope and with a deliberate intention, not uncommon in warfare, had sunk the ships and their crews.

On December 16th, therefore, the public knew that Lord Palmerston had resigned and that a Turkish squadron had been destroyed at Sinope. *The Times* announced that the two incidents were unconnected and that Lord Palmerston's resignation was due to his disagreement with Lord John's Reform Bill. On December 17th *The Morning Post* indignantly denied that Lord Palmerston was opposed to reform and, in company with almost every other paper in the country, declared that his resignation was due to the " un-English " foreign policy of our Government which had allowed Turks to be massacred within a few miles of a British fleet.

3. The Cabinet and Sinope.
(December 14th–22nd)

It was, therefore, during Lord Palmerston's absence that the Cabinet were forced to deal with the new situation created by the incident of Sinope. The news was not unexpected. The peaceful members of the Cabinet had feared that Turkey would hasten a collision with the Russian fleet in order to involve the British fleet on her side. On November 8th, Clarendon had written to Stratford regretting that the promise of the Turks to refrain from hostilities "had not been acted upon," [1] and on the 11th, had heard from Stratford that he had at any rate restrained the Turks from sending their fleet into the open sea.[2] But neither he nor Aberdeen had much confidence in this new promise.

[1] *E.P.*, ii. 218.   [2] Ibid., 252.

The Queen, too, had already anticipated the danger. As early as October 11th, she wrote: " It appears to the Queen that we have taken on ourselves, in conjunction with the French, all the risks of an European war, without having bound Turkey to any conditions with respect to provoking it." [1]

That Turkey intended to provoke it was already clear to Aberdeen on November 20th, when he wrote to the Queen :—

" It appears that Lord Stratford contemplates a hostile collision in the event of the fleet meeting with a Russian force, but even if this should not necessarily be the case, the Turks will take good care to produce it. They care little about the sacrifice of life, and will, undoubtedly, engage the Russian in the presence of the British fleet. It would be impossible for any British officer to see them defeated without rendering them assistance ; and a flagrant act of hostility would be committed against Russia, without any declaration of war or due notice. Something of this kind sooner or later seems to be inevitable." [2]

During the next week news came that some Turkish vessels had actually put out into the Black Sea and the Queen wrote to Aberdeen: " Wherefore should three poor Turkish steamers go to the Crimea, but to beard the Russian fleet, and to tempt it to come out of Sevastopol, which would thus constitute the much desired contingency for our combined fleets to attack it and so engage us irretrievably ? " [3] The Prince Consort agreed : " This can only be meant to insult the Russian fleet, and to entice it to come out in order thereby

[1] Martin, ii. 521.   [2] *Correspondence*, 20/11/53.
[3] *Letters*, ii. 565.

to make it possible for Lord Stratford to bring the fleet into collision." [1]

In the Cabinet the same view seems at first to have prevailed. The Turks had declared war and opened hostilities : no one could expect the Russian fleet to refrain from destroying any Turkish vessels that appeared within reach. The Duke of Argyll, many years afterwards, wrote of his feelings when the disaster of Sinope was announced to him : " The silly and wayward Turks, after declaring war against Russia, had the inconceivable folly to send their little wretched fleet into the Black Sea and to anchor it in the open and undefended harbour of Sinope." [2] But we have also contemporary evidence that this was the general view of the Cabinet. Sinope at first seemed merely an unnecessary and annoying event for which provision had already been made and which required no new policy. On December 17th, three days after the confirmation of the news of Sinope, Clarendon wrote to Stratford that he " had no doubt that the fleet had already entered the Black Sea to protect Constantinople," [3] and on the 20th added that the Government had just determined that no special instructions to the admirals were necessitated by the disaster. It had so far resisted the French proposals for special measures and was animated by an " unabated desire for peace." He informed Lord Stratford that " the course which he was taking with a view to the adoption by the Porte of pacific

---

[1] Martin, ii. 533, 17/11/53.

[2] Argyll, i. 407.

[3] *E.P.*, ii. 330. In accordance with the instructions already given, vide above, 37, Stratford was certainly ready. " You have brought some good news," he said, on receiving the news of Sinope, " for that means *war*. The Emperor of Russia chose to make a personal quarrel with me and now I am avenged." Stanmore, *Aberdeen*, 254.

counsels is in accordance with the wishes of Her Majesty's Government, as being calculated to prepare the Porte to give a favourable reception to the proposals which have been forwarded from Vienna."

Two days later, however, the Cabinet completely altered their policy and accepted the French proposal to announce to the Tsar that "every Russian ship thenceforward met in the Euxine would be requested, and if necessary, contrained to return to Sevastopol: and that any act of aggression afterwards attempted against the Ottoman territory or flag would be repelled by force." [1]

This decision was not a declaration of war but it was a challenge to Russia, and was necessarily fatal to the new peace proposals then on their way to the Tsar. The result was what might have been expected. Count Nesselrode requested an explanation of our demand, asking why the affair at Sinope was styled "wanton aggression," in distinction from any other act of warfare, and further, whether the Black Sea was to be closed to Turkish as well as to Russian ships. The reply was unfavourable and the Russian ambassadors were withdrawn from Paris and London.

This sudden change in the policy of the Government must again be attributed to public opinion. Both in England and in France the disaster of Sinope had roused a demand for immediate hostilities.[2] Lord Aberdeen explained the action of the Cabinet to the Queen with sufficient clearness. "I should," he said, "have hesitated to agree to this proposal had it not been evident that the continu-

---

[1] *E.P.*, ii. 307.
[2] French opinion had not, until Sinope, been excited against the Tsar. Even now it was quiet in comparison with English. Simpson, 243–4.

matum demanding the withdrawal of Russian ships
would make the Tsar's acceptance of the Note
impossible. Kinglake, in commenting on this
decision, makes a remark which shows a keen
observation of Mr. Gladstone's character and
possibly a knowledge of Sir William Molesworth's
note-book.[1] He writes :—

" The proposal seemed made to win the Chancellor
of the Exchequer ; for it fell short of war by a
measure of distance which, though it might seem
very small to people with common eyesight, was
more than broad enough to afford commodious
standing-room to a man delighting as he did in
refinements and slender distinctions."[2]

This decision was taken on December 22nd ;
on the 24th Lord Palmerston returned to office.
Greville, after a conversation with Sir James
Graham, reported that " Palmerston is quite at his
ease and just as if nothing had happened, which
was exactly like him."[3] The Coalition continued
and Lord Palmerston was its most comfortable
member.

4. The Resignation of Lord Palmerston.
(December 14th–24th).

Lord Palmerston's conduct in resigning on
December 14th, and resuming office in the Cabinet
ten days later bewildered contemporary observers
and has not been explained by subsequent historians. Outside the small circle of informed
opinion, his resignation was almost universally
believed to be due to disagreement with his colleagues on the Eastern Question, supplemented by
unconstitutional pressure exerted by the Crown.
In Kinglake's opinion the popular view that Palmerston was a second time a victim to Prince Albert's

[1] Vide above, 163.   [2] Kinglake, ii. 24.   [3] Grev., vii. 124.

interference was correct.[1] Mr. Strachey, who has given by far the most interesting account of the incident, writes : "The cause of Palmerston's resignation, indeed, remains wrapped in obscurity, and it is possible that it was brought about by the continued hostility of the Court.[2]"

The unpublished letters of Lord Aberdeen, without completely clearing the matter up, do enable us to settle some of the difficulties. In the first place, pressure from the Court was almost certainly not the cause of his resignation. Both Albert and the Queen were glad, as indeed they always were, to have Palmerston out of office and would have liked to prevent his return, but Palmerston was the first to suggest his resignation and Aberdeen was prepared to accept it without any interference from the Crown. In December it had become clear that the Cabinet could not remain even nominally united. On the 6th, Aberdeen wrote to the Queen that Palmerston had sent him a letter explaining that he was unable to accept Lord John's Reform Bill and added that " it is by no means improbable that Lord Palmerston may also desire to separate himself from the Government, in consequence of their pacific policy, and in order to take the lead of the war party and the anti-reformers in the House of Commons who are essentially the same. Such a combination would, undoubtedly, be formidable ; but Lord Aberdeen trusts that it would not prove dangerous. At all events, it would tend greatly to the improvement of Lord John's foreign policy."

On the next day the Queen replied : " With respect to Lord Palmerston, the Queen is not

---

[1] Kinglake, ii. 27–32. He speaks mysteriously of " information which he is not at liberty to divulge."

[2] Strachey, 178.

in the eyes of the country by its being thought, either that an intrigue had temporarily succeeded in displacing Lord Palmerston, but that the conviction that the Government could not do without him had obliged them to readmit him, or that such concessions had been made on the Reform Bill as will make the country doubt the sincerity of the intentions of the Cabinet with regard to that question ?

" The Queen would say that Lord Palmerston's character also would suffer under the circumstances, did she not know his unscrupulous dexterity, enabling him to represent himself, even in this instance, as an innocent, injured man whose traducers had been finally obliged to beg him on their knees to come back.

" The fear entertained of Lord Palmerston's power in Opposition has always appeared to the Queen to be unduly exaggerated." [1]

This letter constitutes the nearest approach to royal interference on this occasion. The Queen was here, as always, a strong partisan, and in every case attributed the worst motive to Palmerston and urged her view upon Aberdeen. In spite of her wishes, however, Palmerston returned to office, and the effects of his return were just those which she had feared.

The royal will, then, did not materially affect the situation. We are left with two questions. Firstly, what was the real ground for Palmerston's resignation ? Secondly, why did he return ten days later ? The public universally believed that the disaster at Sinope was the occasion of his departure. But the first rumours of Sinope did not reach England until December 10th, and Palmerston had already expressed his final inability to go further

[1] *Correspondence*, December 21st.

with the Government policy of Reform as early as the 6th. It is, however, possible that distaste for membership in a Cabinet which might not act vigorously even after Sinope, rendered his final decision easier to make.[1]

It is equally difficult to believe that his attitude was solely determined by the Reform Question. He stated that his objection to Lord John's Bill was one of " principle " ; yet he actually returned to the Cabinet without any concessions being made and was willing to accept the Bill in its original form. There can be no doubt that he felt a genuine dislike for the Reform Bill, but he was willing to swallow his objections in the event of agreement on other issues.

The facts appear to be these : Palmerston threatened resignation on both questions. Perhaps he thought Aberdeen would give way on both rather than risk the fall of the Government. In any case he intended to change its policy or to leave it. He told Aberdeen he could go no further with Reform. Aberdeen, as we have seen, wrote immediately to the Queen that Palmerston was likely to resign. He agreed with her Majesty that this was desirable if the cause of his resignation was the unpopular issue of Reform and not the dangerous topic of the Eastern Question. Indeed, so anxious was he to be able to carry out a pacific foreign policy unhindered by Palmerston, that it is possible that he read more eagerness to resign into Palmerston's letter than its writer had intended.[2]

---

[1] He actually resigned on the day of the confirmation of the news of Sinope.

[2] Cp. Reeve, ii. 356. Sir Arthur Gordon (the fourth son of Lord Aberdeen, afterwards Lord Stanmore and that time Governor of Ceylon) wrote to Reeve in 1888, that when in 1853 Palmerston " announced his hostility to Reform, it was determined to take advantage of this announcement to remove him." His further statement

and conscientiously. This letter to Lansdowne
has a little shaken my convictions, but still I am
struck with the fact of his having refrained from
resigning on the Eastern Question, when by so
doing he might have damaged the Government
immensely, and obtained for himself increased
popularity and considerable power if these were
his objects." [1]

Perhaps a measure of praise is due to Palmerston
for not wantonly overthrowing the Government
and destroying the last hope of peace with Russia.
But there is one important point which Greville
overlooked and which the Queen, in discussing
Palmerston's motives for resigning had noticed
but not understood.[2] If Lord Palmerston had
resigned on the Eastern Question Lord John would
probably have followed him. On the Reform
Question, Lord Lansdowne might resign with him,
but clearly Lord John could not. After his dismissal in 1851 Palmerston had always made it
perfectly clear that he would never again serve under
Lord John, even though Lord John was still the
recognized leader of the Whigs. No one had then
thought of Palmerston as a possible Premier during
Russell's lifetime. But whether he had the Premiership in mind or not it is probable that Palmerston
wished for the popularity of resigning from the
most unpopular of Cabinets and did not desire
Lord John to share in that popularity. He wished
to be rid of Lord John. He therefore accepted
Reform as the Cabinet reason for his resignation,
and allowed the country, aided by *The Morning
Post*, to form a different conclusion.

[1] Grev., vii. 116.
[2] Vide above, 175. " Lord Palmerston seems to have thought he
could throw over Lord John also, provided Lord Lansdowne went
with him. . . ."

Out of office, he found that his popularity was even greater than he expected. But Lord Lansdowne had not resigned with him and the Government would be able, at any rate for a time, to continue without him. To turn out the Government he would have to go into Opposition. This is what everyone expected him to do. But in one thing at least Lord Palmerston was consistent—he would not join the Tories. The Tories constantly hoped for his secession, and he was willing to encourage them in their hopes, but he was a Whig and intended to remain one. When he heard that in his absence the Cabinet had adopted the decisive measure against Russia which he had long advocated, it seemed well to resume office. It would naturally be supposed that the Government's change of policy was the price of his return. He allowed his wife and friends to open negotiations, neither asked nor offered any concessions, and wrote to Lord Aberdeen explaining that he had been under a misapprehension as to the Reform Bill. Apparently its provisions were not, as he had thought, " finally settled." His friends in the Government, he said, therefore advised him to " withdraw a resignation which, they assure me, was founded on a misconception on my part.[1]

" You will perhaps allow me to add that the decision, which I am informed the Cabinet came to yesterday, to accede to the proposal of the French Government, whereby the British and French squadrons will have the command of the Black Sea, greatly enters into the consideration[s] which have led me to address this letter to you."[2]

[1] As a matter of fact the Reform Bill had not been discussed since he left the Cabinet when none of its provisions were " finally settled."

[2] *Correspondence*, December 23rd.

Aberdeen's reply showed that he appreciated the humour of the situation and that he was a match for Palmerston in private though Palmerston might win all the public honours.

" As I had communicated your resignation of office to the Queen, I thought it right to take Her Majesty's pleasure before answering your letter received this morning.

" I confess that I cannot well understand how you could infer from my letter of the 14th inst., that the details of the intended Reform Bill had been finally settled by the Government, and that no objection to any part of those details would be listened to, as you were yourself a member of the committee which had not completed its deliberations, when, by your letter to me of the 10th inst., you expressed very decided opinions adverse to all the leading provisions of the proposed measure. However, I wish to say no more upon that which you allow to have been a misconception on your part ; and I very readily agree to consider your letter of the 14th inst., cancelled.

" Although not connected with the cause of your resignation, I am glad to find that you approve of a recent decision of the Cabinet, with respect to the British and French fleets, adopted in your absence. I feel assured you will have learnt with pleasure, that, whether absent or present, the Government are duly careful to preserve from all injury the interests and dignity of the country." [1]

Next day Lord Palmerston returned to the Cabinet. He had gained all round. His popularity was greater than ever. Outside immediate Government circles everyone believed that he had returned on his own terms, though in fact no concession

[1] *Correspondence*, December 24th.

had been made to him. In the war with Russia
he became the most prominent Minister; he
did not join the Tories, he did not serve under
Lord John and, as it happened, he did not even
have to become party to the Reform Bill.[1] After
a short interval he became Prime Minister with
Lord John serving as a member of his Cabinet.

Lady Palmerston was justifiably proud: " He
is always right in everything he does," [2] she said,
and who could contradict her ?

5. The Enlightened Turk.
(Public Opinion—October–December)

The news of the Sultan's ultimatum to the Tsar,
so irritating to Lord Clarendon and his fellow
peacemakers, was greeted with joyous enthusiasm
by the British public. During the autumn and
winter, mass meetings were held in every part
of the country. Almost complete unanimity was
displayed : firstly, in denouncing Lord Aberdeen
for his pro-Russian policy; secondly, in calling
upon Lord Palmerston to conduct the nation to
the aid of Turkey; thirdly, in execrating the Tsar
as the odious oppressor of European liberty, and
lastly, in eulogizing the Sultan as the defender
of Liberalism and the bulwark of Europe against
Russian aggression. Mention of the Sultan himself
now evoked that tumultuous applause usually
reserved by the British public for the triumphant
athlete. The Eastern Question had, indeed, become
a sporting encounter between Russia and Turkey
—with the betting heavily on the latter. But
there were still a few who wondered whether
Turkey might not prove to be the " wrong horse."

[1] Lord John introduced his Reform Bill in March, but as no one
showed any interest in it, it was abandoned.
[2] Grev., vii. 116.

Everywhere abuse of the Tsar alternated with praise of the Sultan. On October 5th, the news that Turkey had offered to declare war was announced to a meeting which had been summoned to inform the Government of its views on the Eastern Question. " Rapturous applause " greeted the announcement, and the chief speaker, Captain Harris, was assured that the public would not " suffer England to fall in the eyes of the Turks," who were " among the most enlightened of European nations, if enlightenment meant high moral principle ? " [1]

At Glasgow an equally enthusiastic meeting was addressed by a Mr. Kennedy who, having been for four years an attendant of the Tsar, offered to give some account of his character. He was, however, hissed off the platform for the incautious statement that " apart from his public character, no man was more affectionate, both as a husband, a father, and a friend." On his attempting to resume, the chairman refused to allow him further to annoy the audience, who had come, he said, " to be enlightened," and not to hear Mr. Kennedy tell stories of the amiability of the Tsar. [2]

On October 7th, a meeting on the Eastern Question was called at the London Tavern. Why, asked a speaker, was our Government not actively helping the Turks ? Because our Government was a weak, vacillating, perhaps treacherous one. " If," he went on, " we had a bold energetic, far-seeing man at the head of affairs [loud cries of ' Palmerston '], yes, if we had such a man as Lord Palmerston I do not think the Russian armies would have crossed the Pruth." When the applause had

[1] Report in *The Globe*, 6/10/53.
[2] Report in *Reynolds's*, 11/12/53.

died away, a member of the audience, mindful of the speeches of Kossuth and the writings of David Urquhart, rose to ask why, in that case, Palmerston had not prevented the Tsar from crushing the Hungarian Revolution in 1849 ? The speaker's answer was accepted with ready enthusiasm. At that time, he pointed out, the Manchester men had been in the ascendant, the Army and Navy had been reduced, and Palmerston would not bark because he knew that England could not bite.[1]

A slightly different answer to the same question was given to two thousand people who had met together in a theatre at Chester. Lord Palmerston had not aided Hungary five years before, said an orator, because he had no support in the country. Then the public had been apathetic : now was the time to demonstrate the truth of Palmerston's declaration that " Public Opinion is more powerful than the charges of cavalry or the thunder of artillery."

At this meeting the Government was charged with refusing information, with continuing negotiations, and attempting to deceive English people into the idea that peace was possible. In fact, declared the principal speaker amid great enthusiasm, the people of England had too little share in the management of foreign affairs, and found that they were not being conducted in a " straight-forward old-English manner." He was ashamed to say that " diplomacy " was afoot : it was a " foreign word, an ambiguous word, a sneaking word." No doubt, he said, there was truth in the idea that men were all brothers, but sometimes even a brother must be treated with a just severity. Russia had forfeited all claim

[1] Report in *M.P.*, 8/10/53.

to fraternal affection. Her treatment of the refugees, her pretence of religious obligation as an excuse for aggression in the Balkans were alone sufficient to cut her off from the family of nations. It was time to marshal the democracies of the world—unfortunately Austria and Sweden would be on the side of tyranny, but France, America, Hungary, and Poland—and a burst of cheering greeted each name—would be on the side of Liberty.

He then proposed a comprehensive resolution which was passed by acclamation : That England should assist the Sultan " by the strongest warlike measures " . . . on the ground that " there is no sovereign in Europe who has higher claims than the Sultan to the support of this country : no sovereign . . . who has done more for religious toleration ; for he has established religious equality in his dominions. It would be no dishonour to Englishmen if they were to rank him with the Alfreds and Edwards : and, if properly supported at the present crisis by the nations of West Europe, he will make his dominions happy and prosperous and establish commercial relations of mutual advantage between them and Great Britain." [1]

It is a curious picture. In a palace on the Bosphorus sat the Sultan, a fleshy and irascible debauchee, usually intoxicated and always lethargic, surrounded by a group of Mohammedan fanatics of whose plots to supplant him he was dimly aware and whose ability to rouse the fury of a priest-ridden mob kept him in abject terror and peevish submission. In England were public halls, crowded with respectable shopkeepers, evangelical maiden ladies, and stolid artisans enthusiastically proffering their lives and money in the service

[1] Report of a meeting at Chester, October 1853.

of this obese little tyrant in a fez, whose name they could not pronounce and whose habits of life were as unknown to them as those of a pre-historic monster.

Yet their conduct was neither exceptional nor irrational. There were merely behaving normally in accordance with their picture of the situation. This picture was a mistaken one built up from past associations; present facts had to fit into it as best they might. Perhaps this is best illustrated by the controversy upon the decadence of Turkey. That Turkey was a decaying power which could not much longer retain her hold upon her Christian subjects had been a common belief put forward by numerous writers. A few pamphlets, restating this opinion, continued to appear during the later months of 1853. "Pacificus" was glad that no treaty bound us to aid Turkey whose declaration of war against Russia relieved us of the "necessity of firing a shot in the cause of unimproving barbarism against progressive civilization." The gradual strengthening of Greece seemed the only solution to the Near Eastern Problem.[1] "Veritas," declaring that Turkey was "sunk in barbarism," gave examples of atrocities committed against the Christians in the Balkans, and added that Russian encroachment was a "bugbear." The only solution was to divide the Turkish Empire harmoniously between England, France, Russia, and Austria.[2] But this point of view became increasingly rare. It was answered in two ways. The first answer was that, if Turkey was weak,

---

[1] "One Word for Russia and Two for Ourselves," by "Pacificus."

[2] "Partition of Turkey, the Indispensable Feature of the Present Political Crisis," by "Veritas." In the same strain of "Remarks on the Present Aspect of the Turkish Question," by a Member of the University of Oxford, June 1853.

there was all the more reason for protecting her against aggression. The second answer was a simple denial. Many books and pamphlets appeared during the later part of the year with one object in view—to prove the reforming spirit in Turkey and to show the weakness of the Tsar. Most influential of these was " The Shores of the Black Sea " by Laurence Oliphant, which went through four editions in six months. Mr. Oliphant declared that Russian strength was much over-estimated, yet this did not prevent her from being dangerous to Turkey and to Europe. Only a small part of the Russian Navy was seaworthy, and so little accustomed were her sailors to their work that they could not navigate a ship in the Black Sea, even in the rare occasions when they were not sea-sick. Their fortress of Sevastopol, so imposing to the eye, was defended with pieces of artillery which could not be fired without bringing down the " rotten batteries." " Lack of communications, climate, and corruption " prevented the Army from being of any account. It was, in fact, merely a " review army "—a glittering " Imperial plaything." And yet, Russia was dangerous. Her hold upon the Black Sea was fatal to trade, her expansion in Asia was a menace to Persia and worse, to India.[1] She was already the great enemy of freedom in Poland and Hungary, while " the next Revolution in France would see Italy occupied by Russian troops." But Russia knew her own weakness, relied on " haughty blustering " and, if attacked, would fall to pieces. The

---

[1] Laurence Oliphant was one of the first to introduce the " Road to India " motive, which appears only occasionally in 1853–4. Morley (*Cobden*, ii. 150) is incorrect in saying it had not yet been invented, but it did not play a principal part in the Crimean period.

Cossacks, bemoaning their ancient freedom, would rise against the Tsar ; Georgia, hostile to her Government, could be enlisted on our side and general revolt would follow. For everywhere, " from the Baltic to the Black Sea, from the shores of the Danube to the banks of the Pheisis, extends an indissoluble bond of sympathy—a deeply rooted hatred of Russia." [1]

This view of the situation was the easily accepted one. It is good to believe in an enemy's weakness. The newspapers which had been largely instrumental in creating the popular image of the Eastern Question must now perforce conform to it. To Mr. Urquhart the excitement in the country was an eloquent testimony to the efficacy of his own articles. " I find," he wrote, " the phrase has become current that I am rousing the democracy of England." [2] *The Morning Post*, without assuming sole responsibility for the soundness of the popular view of the Eastern Question, was sure that only surrender on the Tsar's part could justify the continuation of peace ; [3] it sternly pointed out to him that his conciliatory remarks at Olmütz had come too late,[4] and by the middle of October had become persuaded that there " will be no more Notes." [5] *The Morning Herald* wished to know if it were possible that England was " really again to be humiliated by negotiations." [6] and solemnly warned the Government that " for any Englishman to betray the cause of Turkey is to betray the Queen." [7]

[1] " The Shores of the Black Sea " (1st edition, October 1853, 4th edition, March 1854), pp. 257–60, 320–65. For reviews of other books on Russia and Turkey 1853, cp. *The Edinburgh Review*, January 1854, and *The Westminster Review*, December 1853, where Mr. Urquhart's published articles were examined.
[2] *M. A.*, 29/10/53. [3] 4/10/53. [4] 5/10/53.
[5] 16/10/53. [6] 8/10/53. [7] Quoted *M.A.*, 24/10/53.

In November, the suggestion that the Tsar might still give way, and the announcement that new peace terms were being arranged at Vienna, were both denounced as methods of gaining time for the Tsar ; Austria's duplicity was taken for granted, and a crescendo of enthusiasm greeted the news of Turkish victories. On November 12th a manifesto issued by the Tsar, summoning God to the aid of the True Church against the pagan hosts of Islam was an opportunity for the most scathing flights of editorial satire.[1]

But even now there were papers which refused to conform to the popular image. Peace proposals were still going forward and an uneasy recollection of former accounts of Turkish misrule haunted the columns of *The Manchester Guardian* and *The Morning Chronicle*. The latter, it is true, had ceased to hope for peace, but was always gentle in its treatment of its Governmental patrons and sceptical about the reform of the Ottoman Empire. *The Manchester Guardian* was alone in stating that information from the East was so scanty as to make accurate judgment on these matters impossible.[2] It ridiculed both the enthusiasm evinced for Turkey at the London Tavern meeting and the pretensions of the Peace Society to influence public opinion at their Edinburgh conference.[3] It declared that " everyone is sick of the Eastern Question " and deplored that " even a casual

---

[1] Count Buol's proposal of a new peace Note was announced on the day that the Tsar's manifesto was published. For example of the result vide *M.P.*, 12/10/54.

[2] 14/10/53.

[3] 15/10/53, 22/10/53. The conference was held on October 12th, and was addressed by many Nonconformist M.P.'s and others. Bright and Cobden, who were the most prominent speakers, made lengthy addresses on complete pacifist lines. Most of the other speakers were more cautious.

battle, in the present excited state of feeling would be a deplorable event, exciting a taste for bloodshed." [1]

The Times held the same position. Delane had not yet become one of the public. His intimacy with Cabinet Ministers prevented his sharing the popular delusions of Turkish blamelessness. On October 4th, he " was sent for by Lord Aberdeen " and a long conversation followed in which " Aberdeen told him that he was resolved to be no party to a war with Russia on such grounds as the present, and he was prepared to resign rather than incur such responsibility." [2]

Delane agreed with him that there were as yet no grounds for war, and throughout October *The Times* reiterated that the negotiations were still likely to prove successful. Turkey should, if possible, be restrained from actual hostilities, and the Four Powers could then find a path of " moderation and wisdom " for Russia's retreat.[3] Moreover, Delane was largely in agreement with John Bright, when in an open letter of October 13th, he stated that " war will not save Turkey if peace cannot save her ; but war will brutalize our people, increase our taxes, destroy our industry, and postpone Parliamentary Reform, it may be for years. . . ." [4]

On October 14th, however, came the report of a conference of the Peace Society at Edinburgh. Delane was exceedingly annoyed by the extreme form of pacificism, and *The Times* ridiculed the Quakers as mercilessly as *The Morning Post*.[5]

[1] 9/11/53.   [2] Grev., vii. 95.
[3] *Times*, e.g. October 12th, 13th, 17th, 18th, 21st.
[4] *Times*, 12/10/53.
[5] 14/10/53. *The Manchester Guardian*, 15/10/53, also said that it was " impossible to say too much in reproach of their [the Peace Society's] unteachable vanity."

" comprehensive war." When it came to the
point, the more cautious, though glad that our
fleet was protecting Turkey, feared for our commerce
in the event of an Eastern war, and were anxious
rather to aid the Turks by resolutions at public
meetings than by an expenditure of blood and
treasure. Moreover, during November, it seemed
that the Turks could look after themselves, and
the readiness of our fleet seemed to·be all that
honour required. In October, Mr. Gladstone
found a division of opinion when he addressed a
meeting at Manchester, and wrote to Aberdeen
that he was inclined to think the peace party
" decidedly the stronger." [1] In fact, before Sinope,
though the picture of Russian guilt and Turkish
heroism was clear, there was no event round which
public sentiment could crystallize. The British
public was not yet convinced that the interests
of Christianity or the safety of the Empire demanded
an immediate declaration of war. The moral
motive was still lacking. This need was supplied
by the news of the engagement at Sinope. On
the same day Lord Palmerston's resignation was
made public. The effect of this double announcement was overwhelming. Seldom, if ever, in
English history has public sentiment run so high
or so menacingly as it did during the month that
followed. For now the popular picture of the
Eastern situation was completed, and the most
horrible conjectures of the imagination of David
Urquhart seemed justified. The Tsar, already the
incarnate soul of evil, had once more put forth
his hand to torture and destroy : the Sultan,
victorious hero though he might be, was hard
pressed in the fight with darkness : England,
pledged to his assistance, had stood idly by and

[1] *Correspondence*, 12/10/53.

watched the massacre of his sailors. Our national honour was trailed in the dust and our Ministers proved to be treacherous agents of the Tsar. Among them there had been one man whom the people had trusted, one English gentleman who would never betray his country. And he, in verification of every fear, was driven from office!

Divisions of opinion as to the need of war with Russia now disappeared. *The Times, The Globe, The Chronicle,* and *The Manchester Guardian* all put aside their doubts. All the niceties of the subject, all the fear that Turkey was not worth fighting for, all the forebodings about our commerce and hesitations about Christianity—all were swept away. *The Manchester Guardian,* which was least affected by the popular frenzy, admitted that war was "inevitable." [1] *The Globe* was at first so sure that Turkey was fighting a victorious war that it refused to believe that Russian ships could have destroyed Turkish ones. The story of Sinope, therefore, was a piece of Russia's boastfulness. On the 14th, therefore, it declared that details had come to hand showing that an immensely superior Russian force, although victorious, came out of the engagement "in a scarcely less shattered condition than its opponents." A few days later, when it became impossible to doubt that Sinope was a Turkish disaster, an editorial complained that " our statesmen (and we do not in the least except the regretted Lord Palmerston) have been too much in the habit of transacting business with Russia as if Russia were accessible to the ordinary motives of the rest of the European family." [2]

The Morning Chronicle suffered a similar change. On the staff there was only one writer who doubted.

[1] 24/12/53. [2] 20/12/53.

of his resignation, which, unlike *The Times*, they found a source of bewilderment and regret.[1] But no one believed them.[2] *The Morning Post*, under the guidance of Palmerston himself, led the attack on this new proof of Governmental treachery. Lord Palmerston did not tell Mr. Borthwick that he had resigned on foreign policy ; he left *The Morning Post* to draw the natural conclusion. On December 16th, he wrote to Mr. Borthwick :—

" *The Times* of to-day asserts that I have left the Government because I am opposed to all measures of Parliamentary reform. I wish you would say in the *Post* that this is entirely untrue ; that, on the contrary, I have been ready to agree to a very considerable measure of reform though I did not choose to be a party to proposing to Parliament measures of change which, in my opinion, went beyond the necessities of the time and which I thought inexpedient. You may add that it is equally untrue that my objections were not stated plainly and distinctly from the first moment when the measures to which they were related were proposed and discussed. State this, not from authority, but as what you have good reason to believe." [3]

This was sufficient for Mr. Borthwick. The next morning *The Morning Post* announced that *The Times* was " utterly false " in saying that Lord Palmerston was not a Reformer : that he was willing to accept a moderate Reform Bill and had, as a matter of fact, resigned on the Eastern Question. On the 19th, this was repeated with more vehemence, and

[1] 16/12/53.

[2] *The Manchester Guardian*, 17/12/53, came nearest to accepting *The Times* statement ; no other paper even considered their explanation possible. It was clear that they scarcely believed themselves.

[3] Glenesk, 139.

on the 20th, an editorial declared that the Cabinet would be helpless without Lord Palmerston, whose motives for resigning were clear in spite of officially inspired untruths in *The Times*. " Everyone will judge for himself according to his estimate of the man." [1] On the 22nd, numerous letters and extracts from provincial papers were quoted showing that the public had judged—according to their estimate of the man. " The English public," *The Post* declared, " knows the real reason why Palmerston has resigned." It was the same cause which had driven him from office in 1851. It was due to an unseen power behind the Ministry— a " *rapprochment* between the Courts of Vienna and England."

The hunt was up. Every paper recalled the incident of Lord Palmerston's former dismissal : he had favoured France when the Crown wished to please the Tsar and the Austrian Emperor. A letter to *The Morning Post* led the way. It was intolerable that we should still allow this foreign influence in high places. Why do Englishmen tolerate " the swarm of northern intriguers which luxuriates in our palaces and blocks up the ingress by which good old English truth and feeling, sometimes at least, might find its way to the throne." [2]

The Daily News, mindful of Palmerston's past inconsistency towards Liberal movements, thought him too unprincipled to deserve whole-hearted praise, but reminded its readers of his dismissal in 1851, and added that " some of his admirers may even go so far as to hint that Courtly distastes and Coburg intrigues " were again responsible. To *The Morning Herald* it seemed that " now, as it was two years ago, the exclusion of Lord

[1] *M.P.*, 17th, 19th, 20th.   [2] *M.P.*, 22/12/53.

since the Government could not get on without
him, Palmerston had gone back on the assurance
that the coming war against Russia would be
properly conducted.[1] Other papers, not troubled
with hints from Lord Palmerston himself, assumed
that " the Noble Viscount has obtained his own
terms ; " " there was nothing left for it [the
Ministry] to do but to eat the humblest pie :
everything was conceded to Lord Palmerston
would he only condescend to return."[2] *The Press*
had, as usual, an unusual way of expressing the
common opinion. On December 24th, it described
the imaginary Cabinet meeting which had invited
Lord Palmerston to return :—

" Lord Aberdeen moved that it was very dis-
agreeable weather. Carried Nem. Con. (with an
addition by Mr. Gladstone that we ought to be
very thankful to Providence that we had any
weather at all). . . . Lord Aberdeen moved, Sir
James Graham seconded, and it was carried
by seven to four (Sir C. Wood, by mistake,
voting both ways) that a message be sent to
Lord Palmerston offering to surrender everything if he would, by returning to office,
save the Coalition Ministry from its inevitable
doom."

With Lord Palmerston's return to the Ministry
it might have been expected that the national
excitement would have decreased. Would not
the suggestion of " treachery in High Places "
cease now that the supposed victim was reinstated ?[3]

[1] 26/12/53.
[2] *M.H.*, December 27th and 28th.
[3] So Mr. Strachey has assumed (Strachey, 184). " Within a few
weeks Palmerston withdrew his resignation, and the public frenzy
subsided as quickly as it had arisen." This is incorrect. Palmerston was out of office for ten days (December 14th to 24th) ; the

The reverse was the case. The newspapers hungered after a scandal. The public was too deeply roused to be appeased thus easily. Everywhere it scented plots : every foreigner might be a Russian spy. Palmerston's return to office was only proof that the public had been right. Clearly he had been reinstated because the " hidden power " was frightened by the voice of the people. But the people were not deceived : they would hunt down the traitor, drag him into the light, and deal with him according to his deserts. So it was that, after Palmerston's return, the hunt became more vigorous and the charges more definite. The newspapers which, in December, had raised the hue and cry upon " Court influence " and " foreign intrigue," in January, were hot upon the trail of a " certain illustrious personage," " one occupying the Highest Place in the realm " ; finally, they cast aside the last disguise and, with a shriek of triumph, fell upon their prey. The traitor was Prince Albert.

7. The Attack on Prince Albert.
(December–January)

It was inevitable that the Prince Consort should be selected as the popular victim. The logic of the matter was simple and irrefutable ; the circumstantial evidence perfect. The facts, as it happened, were illogical and the circumstantial evidence pointed to a wrong conclusion. But who could believe this ? Albert, notoriously a foreigner, friendly to European Governments, whose

" public frenzy " lasted until February and was at its height in January.

It was the meeting of Parliament, and the fact that war was obviously about to break out, that pacified the papers at the end of January.

the " English monarchy to a height of power, stability, and symmetry " which it had never attained, at any rate since the reign of George III.[1]

Thus the agitation, beginning in the least respectable papers, was taken up in many unexpected quarters, and for a brief moment even *The Times* admitted that Albert's position was anomalous. The charges against the Prince were promiscuous and extensive. *The Morning Advertiser* led the attack, *The Daily News, The Morning Herald* and *Standard, Reynolds's Weekly,* and *Bell's Life* followed. An extensive pamphlet controversy arose, public meetings denounced the Prince, and " halfpenny broadsides, hawked through the streets of London, re-echoed in doggerel vulgarity the same sentiments and the same suspicions." [2]

From the beginning, *The Morning Advertiser* and *The Morning Herald* declared that it was only owing to special efforts on the part of the Court that Albert's treachery had not been held up to ignominy two years before. Lord John Russell, said *The Herald*, had dismissed Lord Palmerston in 1851 without telling Parliament that " *there was a third key to the dispatch box* which conveyed the papers from the Minister to the Queen." [3] *The Morning Advertiser* offered to be more explicit. The editor possessed an incriminating pamphlet written from documents " coming, as we know that a portion of them do come, either from a certain noble Lord himself, or from someone intimately acquainted with his affairs." This pamphlet would show that the Prince was always in the room when Ministers were engaged in the most confidential discussions, that he enjoyed a special correspondence with England's repre-

[1] Strachey, 178–84.   [2] Ibid., 177.
[3] 9/1/54.

sentatives abroad,[1] and was in constant and traitorous communication with foreign Courts. It would prove up to the hilt his collusion with Vienna : there had been rejoicing at the Austrian Court at Palmerston's dismissal before the news was announced even in England. It further added that the author of the pamphlet, Mr. William Coningham, had been offered a "bribe of £100 and a cask of sherry," for its suppression. On January 19th, Mr. Coningham's article was printed in *The Morning Advertiser*, and *The Times*, by way of throwing ridicule on the accusations, also published it five days later.[2] It was found to contain undocumented insinuations that a plot against the Foreign Minister had been hatched between the English Court and Vienna ; a panegyric of Lord Palmerston and some unpleasant remarks about Lord John Russell. It further asked : "What personage, however high, dares to usurp the authority of a Minister of State ? "

This was enough proof of Albert's guilt. *Reynolds's Weekly* expressed itself satisfied. The foreign policy of this country was entirely ruled by foreigners. "The Prince Prime Minister apparently thinks that none but Germans have the right or title to interfere in the government of this country." In any case, said *The Daily News*, it was impossible for Prince Albert ever to become "an English Liberal." It was obvious that he was "so nurtured and entangled with family connections that he should be forced to

[1] 14/1/54. "If Stratford or Westmorland were asked to give account of their correspondence with Prince Albert. . . ."

[2] *M. A.*, 19/1/54, *Times*, 24/1/54. It was also published bound with another pamphlet, under the title of *Palmerston aud Prince Albert*. Cp. also *Prince Albert's Defence*, written in answer.

Lord Palmerston disclaimed all knowledge of Coningham's pamphlet in *The Morning Post*, 23/1/54.

if somewhat promiscuously underlined, show how
deeply the scurrilous vulgarity of her subjects
had affected her. She read every paper and
pamphlet she could obtain, and was anxious to
know the authorship of any written on the Prince's
behalf. At the height of the onslaught she had
thoughts of desperate measures and came near
to refusing to open Parliament in person. On
January 4th she wrote to the Premier :—

"The Queen had hoped that the scandalous
attacks which had appeared immediately after the
resignation of Lord Palmerston against the Prince,
in several (though none of the *most* respectable)
papers would cease, and, indeed, *had* done so,
but she has been mistaken ; she perceives that
a *systematic* and *most infamous* attack appears
daily in *The Morning Herald* and *Standard*, and
she, therefore, can no longer *doubt* that there is
some design in *this*, which, as Lord Aberdeen will
easily believe, she DEEPLY *resents*."

She felt that the more serious charges should
be met : Albert should be given a Constitutional
position.

"Therefore, upon mature reflection, and after
considering the question for nearly eleven years,
I have come to the conclusion (and I know the
Prince has also) that the *Title* which is now by
universal consent given him of ' *Prince Consort* '
with the highest rank in and out of Parliament,
IMMEDIATELY after the Queen, and before EVERY
OTHER PRINCE of the Royal Family, should be
the one assigned to the *HUSBAND* of the QUEEN
REGNANT *once and for all*." [1]

Lord Aberdeen was sympathetic and believed
that the attack would die down. *The Times*, at
any rate, represented serious opinion and would

[1] *Correspondence*, January 4th and 5th.

take no part in the agitation. But Delane was not sufficiently cautious. In defending Prince Albert he admitted difficulties in the Prince Consort's constitutional position.

This wrung another letter from the Queen, who complained that the Government had allowed even *The Times* to print a " very injudicious article." " If the country," she proceeded " *really has* such incomprehensible and reprehensible notions there is no remedy but the introduction of the *Salic Law*, for which *she* would *heartily* vote. A *woman must have* a support and an adviser ; and *who can* this *properly* be but her husband, *whose duty it is to watch over her interests private and public*. From this *sacred* duty, NO EARTHLY POWER can absolve him ! Were it not for the Prince, the Queen's health and strength would long since have sunk under the multifarious duties of her position as Queen and the mother of a large family. Were the Queen to *believe* that these unprincipled and immoral insinuations really were those of *any* but a wicked and despicable few, she would LEAVE a position which nothing but her domestic happiness could make her endure, and retire to private life—leaving the country to choose another ruler after their own HEARTS' CONTENT. But she does *not* think so ill of her country, though she must say that these disgraceful exhibitions will leave behind them *very bitter* feelings in her breast, which time alone can eradicate !

" If the whole *is* brought before Parliament, which would be better but which seems almost doubtful now, the Queen hopes it will be on the first *night* of the Session, and done with.

" The Queen encloses an extract from her journal of the year 1841, giving *Lord Melbourne's* opinion the Derbyite papers. This led to violent repudiations and counter assaults by Disraeli, Lord Derby, and the Earl of Malmesbury. The only thing that emerged quite clearly from the debate was that no member of either House believed in the guilt of the Prince Consort.[1] The Queen was more than satisfied : " The position of my beloved Lord and Master," she said, " has been defined once and for all." [2] This, however, was exactly the reverse of the fact. All were agreed that the Prince was an excellent husband : possibly he might be considered a royal private secretary ; certainly he was a legal Privy Councillor. Beyond that, however, it was deemed well, according to the best traditions of the British Constitution, to leave definition in a convenient obscurity.

[1] Hansard, cxxx. 74–107, 182–95.　　　　[2] Martin, ii. 563.

CHAPTER VIII

THE EVE OF WAR

(January–March, 1854)

1. Self-persuasion and Self-reproach.

AFTER the engagement of Sinope and the Cabinet decision to demand the withdrawal of Russian ships from the Black Sea, the final negotiations at Vienna were not likely to receive serious consideration in England. The publication of the Tsar's conversation with Sir George Seymour anticipating the decease of the " sick man of Europe," was everywhere received as proof that Russia had long been preparing for the war. The Earl of Shaftesbury told the House of Lords that it was his " deliberate conviction that this was a long-conceived and gigantic scheme, determined on years ago, and now to be executed, for the prevention of all religious freedom, and so ultimately of all civil freedom, among millions of mankind." [1] The secret protocol of 1844, in which the Duke of Wellington, among others, had agreed that the Ottoman Empire could not long be preserved, was not generally known, but if it had appeared

---

[1] Hansard, cxxxi. 593. Cp. the popular song—
" And did he say the Turk was sick
And that the Turk should die ?
There's 50,000 Englishmen
Will know the reason why ! "
                              " War Verses."

equipping the fleet and wrote : " I do not think peace is any longer possible. The Emperor must fight ; and if he pockets our hostile message to Sevastopol, we must send our ultimatum to St. Petersburg." [1]

Sidney Herbert desired to hasten the ultimatum for quite a different reason. He began at last to share the popular view that Russia would seize Constantinople before we were ready to protect it.[2]

" The important point of this opinion," he wrote, " is that which refers to the question of time. Whoever gets the position first will hold it. If once Russia reaches it and captures it all the combined forces could do would be to blockade her from the Mediterranean. Everything must depend on the rapidity with which the troops of France and England can be carried to the scene of action. . . . There is great risk that when our troops arrive at the Dardanelles they may find themselves too late."

The Duke of Argyll remained pacific until the last moment. In *The Edinburgh Review* of July 1854 he described the negotiations and gave the reasons for his final conversion to a war policy. The justification for our ultimatum, he said, was that the Tsar had refused the allied terms which reached him at the same time as the demand that he should evacuate the Black Sea.[3] He further complained that the Tsar laid it down as a condition that he should conduct the final negotiations directly with Turkey.

[1] Maxwell, ii. 37–8. (The italics are in the original.)

[2] Stanmore, *Herbert*, i. 221. He seems to have been converted to this view by reading the *Voyage de Marmont, duc de Raguse*, Trans. 1854. Marshall Marmont had been greatly impressed with the strength of the new fortifications of Constantinople.

[3] Vide above, 42.

" Not only," he writes, " did he spurn the proffered terms of peace, but as if on purpose to set at ease the most peaceful amongst us, he asserted roundly the very doctrine of his own exclusive right to deal with Turkey as he pleased, which we were all united in resisting, and which in principle he had himself repudiated in signing the Treaty of 1840. This was the only issue which justified, in my opinion, a war, nominally in defence of the Turk, but really a war in defence of the right of Europe to keep the fate of Turkey as a matter of common interest and concern." [1]

The condition laid down by the Tsar that, after all, the questions at issue should have been decided by the Four Powers, the actual terms of his treaty with Turkey should be the subject of direct negotiation with the Sultan, has here become " the right to deal with Turkey as he pleased." It had " set at ease the most peaceful of us." But he had forgotten Mr. Gladstone.

What was it that set Mr. Gladstone at ease with himself ? Mr. Gladstone's conscience was a difficult one to satisfy. It was the knowledge of this that made his decision in favour of war so important. " None but a bold man," wrote Kinglake, " could say that the war was needless or wicked whilst Mr. Gladstone was feeding it with his own hand." [2]

Mr. Gladstone himself always denied that the Cabinet " drifted into the war." Was he not a member of it ? " As a member of the Aberdeen Cabinet," he told Lord Morley in 1881, " I never can admit that divided opinions in that Cabinet led to hesitating action or brought on the war." [3] But on February 22, 1854, in conversation with Lord Aberdeen, who could not reconcile himself to

---

[1] Argyll, i. 468. [2] Kinglake, ii. 67.
[3] Morley, *Gladstone*, i. 491–2.

war, Mr. Gladstone gave some hint of his state of mind before the ultimatum.

"He [Lord Aberdeen] asked: 'How could he bring himself to fight for the Turks?' I said we were not fighting for the Turks, but we were warning Russia off forbidden ground. . . . He said if I saw a way to get him out, he hoped I would mention it to him. I replied that my own views of war so much agreed with his, and I felt such a horror of bloodshed, that I thought the matter over incessantly myself. We stand, I said, upon the ground that the Emperor has invaded countries not his own, inflicted wrong on Turkey, and what I feel much more, most cruel wrong on the wretched inhabitants of the Principalities: that war had ensued and was raging with all its horrors; we had procured for the Emperor an offer of honourable terms of peace which he had refused : that we were not going to extend the conflagration (but I had to correct myself as to the Baltic), but to apply more power for its extinction, and this I hoped in conjunction with all the great Powers of Europe."

These seemed good reasons, and yet Mr. Gladstone was haunted by a remaining doubt. What if fighting against Russia should involve us in hostilities with other enemies of the Sultan? What if the Christian subjects of the Sultan revolted? Mr. Gladstone's conscience could stand it no longer. If this should happen he would refuse to support the war. "I, for one, could never shoulder the musket against the Christian subjects of the Sultan and must there take my stand." [1] As it

---

[1] *The Guardian*, which was representative of Mr. Gladstone's religious views, said, on December 21st, that we must always side with the oppressed against the strong and aggressive, but that if the question of helping Turkey against her Christian subjects arose it would be difficult to know what to do. The only solution was to help Turkey now and reform her as the price of our aid.

turned out the muskets were shouldered by those who felt the difficulties of the situation less acutely than Mr. Gladstone.

Lord Aberdeen remained unconvinced even after this conversation. He stood alone, without comfort, and spoke his mind with a kind of bitter courage, which did not hide his self-reproach. Desperately clinging to the hope that the mission of Count Orloff at Vienna would succeed, he was met with derision and abuse even amongst his own colleagues.

" George," wrote Lady Clarendon in her journal, " told him he was humbugging the country by giving it hopes of peace for which there was no real hope, and that if Lord A. did not modify what he had said by informing the House that negotiations were now over he would get up and say so himself ; to which Lord A. said : ' No, no ; I will do it,' which he did. The appearance of vacillation produced an unpleasant laugh in the House." [1] But though he might vacillate about the hopefulness of negotiation in which the Cabinet was not taking a direct part, his feeling about the war was stated with an openness which led to a noble Lord's declaration that " it was no smiling matter when the same doctrines were preached by the head of the Government that were held up by that little club of ridiculous people [the Peace Society]." [2] " The people of this country," Lord Aberdeen had declared, " are not sufficiently impressed with the importance and

[1] Maxwell, ii. 40. Bright, in his journal, records that he had a conversation with Aberdeen and Granville on February 8th. Both still hoped for peace and agreed that Russia was only seeking " influence," and that Turkey had deliberately brought on the war in the knowledge that England and France were committed to her support. Trevelyan, G. M., 230.

[2] Criticism by Lord Beaumont, February 24th, of Lord Aberdeen's speech of February 14th. Hansard, cxxx. 1209.

magnitude of the war in which they may be engaged.
. . . In fact, we have been so long without having
experienced the horrors and miseries of war that
it is but too common to look upon it now as a
source of pleasurable excitement : and I verily
believe that, if by the blessing of God and our
endeavours, we should still be enabled to preserve
peace, a very great disappointment will ensue in
some quarters. I agree in thinking the public
feeling in this matter is a generous feeling . . .
but, my Lords, it is not for us to encourage that
feeling. It is, on the contrary, the duty of the
Government as much as possible to resist such
feelings, however natural and generous they may
be—to direct them in the course of prudence and
of policy. . . . The noble Earl has been pleased to
say that I have been more a War Minister than I
intended or fancied that I should be. In saying
so, he has perhaps spoken more truth than he
intended : for I can assure him that if I have
any misgivings about the course which has been
pursued it is certainly not that we have been too
pacific." [1]

Conscious of the fact that he was obeying and
not leading the people he yet remained in office,
struggling for peace and feeling that it would be
dishonourable to resign. On February 22nd, he
suggested to Mr. Gladstone that " he might himself
withdraw from office when he came to the declaration of war. All along he had been acting against
his feelings, but still defensively. He did not
think that he could regard the offensive in the
same light and was disposed to retire. . . . All
wars were called, or pretended to be, defensive." [2]
The events of the last year had become a night-
mare to him. Who was to blame ? Had there

[1] Hansard, cxxx. 646–8.   [2] Morley, *Gladstone*, i. 491–2.

not been some moment in the negotiations when more loyalty on the part of his colleagues or, more terrible to believe, more firmness on his own part, would have prevented this unspeakable calamity ?

" I believe," he wrote to Lord John in March, " that there were, in the course of the negotiations, two or three occasions when, if I had been supported, peace might have been honourably and advantageously secured. I will especially refer to the opportunity afforded by the transaction which took place at the meeting of the Emperors at Olmütz. But I repeat that the want of support, although it may palliate, cannot altogether justify to my own conscience the course which I pursued." [1]

And again he wrote :—

" The abstract justice of the cause, although indisputable, is but a poor consolation for the inevitable calamities of all war, or for a decision which I am not without fear may prove to have been impolitic and unwise. My conscience upbraids me the more because, seeing as I did from the first all that was to be apprehended, it is possible that, by a little more energy and vigour, not on the Danube, but in Downing Street, it might have been prevented." [2]

As time passed the burden of responsibility grew no less. Haunted with a vision of the reality of war, he told Bright in March that " his grief was such that he felt as if every drop of blood that would be shed would rest upon his head." And, more than a year later, when the tale of tragedy in the Crimea had surpassed his most terrible foreboding, he could find no peace in the thought that time after time he had meant to be firm, had sought a place to " dig his toes in," had at least tried to serve his country. Events had been

[1] *Correspondence*, 3/3/54.   [2] Ibid., 3/3/54.

too big for him. But people, he said, are not to be forgiven on the ground of good intentions, and he himself, who had meant well, was " the greatest culprit of all." [1]

2. A Representative Parliament.

The Cabinet declared war without enthusiasm. It was an evil which they could no longer avoid and which at best could be justified on the ground that the Balance of Power necessitated defence of Turkey. Diplomatic methods would have been sufficient had not public opinion driven the Ministry into a false position from which a variety of accidents had prevented their escape. At any rate they had the consolation offered them by *The Westminster Review* : " While the nation and Parliament are shortsighted, responsible Ministers cannot afford to be longsighted." [2]

In the country there were many individuals who, like the pacific majority in the Cabinet, considered the war an evil which might have been avoided. They expressed this opinion in private conversation and in letters to friends, but beyond that they were silent. Delane, now urging hostilities in *The Times*, privately agreed with Bright that the war was " unnecessary," and Mr. Walter admitted that *The Times* had been " browbeaten into support of the war." " He said," wrote Bright after their conversation, " when a country would go for war, it was not worth while to oppose it, hurting themselves and doing no good." [3] There were others in less responsible positions who, through unusual knowledge or a critical turn of mind, refused to accept the popular view. They felt

[1] Trevelyan, G. M., 232.   [2] Vol. 60, 564.
[3] Trevelyan, G. M., 233.

with Mr. Walter that it was not worth while hurting themselves by opposing war which they could not prevent. Lord Macaulay, who had, in the past, been a vigorous supporter of Palmerston, was present at a debate in which Bright protested, not only against the war, but also against the flippant and lighthearted way in which Palmerston, Graham, and Molesworth had spoken of it at a farewell dinner to Sir Charles Napier. He wrote : " I heard Bright say everything that I thought, and heard Palmerston and Graham expose themselves lamentably. Palmerston's want of temper, judgment, and good breeding was almost incredible. I came home quite dispirited." [1] Sir George Cornwall Lewis, at this time editing *The Edinburgh Review*, wrote : " I think both parties are in the wrong, Russia in making unjust demands, Turkey in resisting a reasonable settlement. My own belief is that England has little or nothing to fear from a Russian occupation of Constantinople, but this is a heresy which it is scarcely safe to utter." [2] So *The Edinburgh Review* decided that the Tsar only was to blame, and heresy was left to the Quakers. Mr. Monckton Milnes, too, suffered from the discomfort of knowing too much. " I heartily wish that I had never seen anything of the East," he wrote to Justin Macarthy, " then I might have formed the clear, decisive, intelligible opinion on one side or the other which politicians and newspapers are enabled to do by reason of their ignorance ; but I am really thankful as it is that my

[1] Quoted ibid., 234, vide Hansard, 13/3/54. Palmerston was called to order for speaking of Bright as the " honourable and 'reverend ' member." For the dinner in honour of Sir Charles Napier at the Reform Club, vide Ashley, ii. 55–9. Ashley explains that " it was the common-sense view of patriotism to neglect no means, however trifling, of keeping up the heart and spirit of the nation."

[2] Lewis, 274.

opinions on the subject have not the slightest weight in the balance."[1]

The bustle of war penetrated even the "sound-proof room" in Cheyne Walk, where Thomas Carlyle, labouring at the first volume of *Frederick the Great*, made a characteristic note in his diary : " Russian war : soldiers marching off, etc. Never such enthusiasm among the population. Cold, I, as a very stone to all that : seems to me privately I have hardly seen a madder business. . . . A lazy, ugly, sensual, dark fanatic that Turk, whom we have now had for 400 years. I, for my part, would not buy the continuance of him there at the rate of sixpence a century. . . . It is the idle population of editors, etc., that have done all this in England. One perceives clearly the Ministers go forward in it against their will. Indeed, I have seen no rational person who is not privately very much inclined to be of my opinion : all fools and loose-spoken inexperienced persons being of the other opinions. Poor Souls ! What could the Ministry *do* after all ? "

And what could he do ? Struggle still more valiantly with the " stupefying chaos " of the eighteenth century, lest he, too, should share the madness of the world.[2]

A number of individuals, then, refused to accept the popular image of the Eastern situation, but there was no political group which opposed the war. Even the Peace Society had given way. Most of its members were either dumb or apologetic.[3] Only the Society of Friends continued to work for peace, and, in January, in despair of influencing

[1] Reid, i. 485.
[2] Froude, ii. 151 ff.
[3] Cp. Miall, 189–90. Edward Miall's views had changed since his speech at the Peace Conference in October.

opinion at home, a deputation of Quakers was
sent to Russia. They were received with courtesy
by the Tsar and with patriotic opprobrium at home.
But neither the Tsar nor the British public seem
to have been greatly influenced by what *The Times*
called, " this piece of enthusiastic folly." [1]

Parliament presented a curious spectacle. The
divisions of the Don Pacifico debate had disappeared. In the Lords, only Earl Grey protested
against the abandonment of England's policy of
non-intervention for one of " knight-erranty " on
behalf of Turkey. In the Commons, Cobden spoke
vigorously against the war, and Bright opposed it
with all the power of sincere and eloquent passion.
The Derbyites had hoped to defeat the Government
at the opening of the session and Disraeli was
" furious " with the war because it had saved the
Administration.[2] The Tories, therefore, attacked
the Government for having made an unnecessary
" Coalition war," and then abused it because,
having rendered war inevitable, it still strove for
peace. Finally, they offered their whole-hearted
co-operation in the coming struggle.

Whigs and Tories, then, were united in demanding
immediate war with Russia. But there was no
agreement as to its justification or its objects.
Some declared that the war would never have
come had there been a firm policy in the Cabinet :
others believed that Russia had determined to go
to war in any case and had been preparing the war
ever since the time of Peter the Great. One speaker
began his speech by saying that " the Government

---

[1] Richard, 464–80. The deputation consisted of Sturge, Pease,
and Charleton. They were afterwards accused in many quarters
of causing the war by encouraging the Tsar to think that England
would not fight. Cp. Kinglake, ii. 53.

[2] Buckle, iii. 540.

had shown no reason why the people of England should go to war," went on to declare that we were "about to enter upon a religious war" for the Holy Places "led by that author of all mischief, the Pope," and ended by demanding that England should "strike a blow at the heart of Russia and proclaim the re-establishment of the Kingdom of Poland." [1] Other members variously claimed that the war was to avenge the massacre of Sinope, to preserve the Balance of Power, the independence and integrity of the Sublime Porte, the rights and the freedom of the Christian minorities in the Ottoman Empire, to give liberty to the democracies of Hungary and Poland, to secure the freedom of the Straits, the honour of the British Empire, the triumph of might against right, and of civilization against barbarism.

These ideas sprang naturally to the minds of those who saw before them the popular image of Russia's aggression, Turkey's heroism, and Palmerston's leadership. Facts seemed annoying and unnecessary. "What they [the people] know and see," said one speaker, "is that there is a big fellow bullying a little one and that the little one is making a brave fight of it—and they are all for the little one. And that is very good and right; but it has nothing to do with the question of the justice of the origin of the war." [2] Under these circumstances it was, in Sir James Graham's phrase,

---

[1] Hansard, cxxx. 971–81. Speech of Mr. Drummond.

[2] Ibid., 1240. Prince Albert's diagnosis was similar. "The Government," he explained to the King of the Belgians, "is a popular Government, and the masses upon which it rests only feel, and do not think. In the present instance their feeling is something of this sort : ' The Emperor of Russia is a tyrant, and the enemy of all liberty on the Continent, the oppressor of Poland. He wanted to coerce the poor Turk. The Turk is a fine fellow ; he has braved the rascal, let us rush to his assistance.' " Quoted Cam. Hist., ii. 374.

unnecessary to " potter over blue books." Exact reasons for the war were irrelevant : the country demanded leadership against a bully. " Wherever I go," said Lord Dudley Stuart, " I have heard but one opinion on the subject, and that one opinion has been pronounced in a single word, or in a single name—Palmerston." [1]

Lord Palmerston himself was ready to lead. The war he declared was to be fought for European liberty.

" Russia, bestriding the Continent from north to south, would become dangerous to the liberties of Europe, and her power would be fatal to the independence of other States. It is a noble sight to see England and France, two countries which for centuries have been in rivalry with each other, now united in a common course of action—bound by reciprocal engagements, and having in view as the result of their operations no selfish advantage—not armed for the purpose of conquest ; not for the oppression of mankind but in a noble cause to defend right against might, and justice against oppression."

Other speakers were no less certain. " The feeling prevails among men of all classes," said another speaker, " not arising from what my Hon. Friend the Member for Manchester has termed the innate bellicose spirit of Englishmen, but from far higher and nobler feelings, the conviction that we are about to be engaged in a great struggle in support of right against wrong and for the maintenance of principles upon which our material interests, as well as the cause of civilization and liberty itself, may depend." Why hesitate further ? " Surely," cried Bulwer Lytton, " if there ever was a war waged on behalf of posterity it is the

[1] Hansard, cxxx. 885.

war which would check the ambition of Russia, and preserve Europe from the outlet of barbarian tribes that require but the haven of the Bosphorus to menace the liberty and the civilization of races as yet unborn ; . . . a war fought, not for our own generation, but that the liberties of our children may be secured from some future Attila and civilization guarded from the irruptions of Scythian hordes."

3. War Ideals.

Parliament, notoriously a representative body, was voicing the opinions expressed in pamphlets, verses, letters, and newspapers throughout the country. The forces of barbarism were led by the Tsar and his Scythian hordes : the forces of civilization by Palmerston and the troops of Turkey, England, and France.[1] The picture of the Tsar as the incarnation of evil at the head of the hosts of darkness was every day more vividly portrayed : terrible descriptions of the punishment of the knout [2] and accounts of cruelties committed by Cossacks on the inhabitants of the Principalities appeared daily in the papers. When the war had actually begun, rumours of Russian atrocities in the Crimea added a new horror to the picture. British soldiers became crusaders fighting with powers more than human. One writer describes the onslaught of the Russian Army : " Then comes the horrid image of a secret, stealthy, creeping mass, slowly dragging its enormous bulk like

[1] One pamphleteer asks : " Does it follow, then, that because Russia is the champion of Evil, Turkey is the representative of the principle of Good ? " a question he seems unable to answer. *The Powers of Europe and the World's Great Quarrel.*

[2] Cp. e.g. *Reynolds's,* 19/3/54.

some reptile, towards that noble, that devoted band of paladins." [1]

Russia, though terrible, seemed easy to defeat. " Charley Napier " would soon finish off the Tsar : everyone knew that Russians could not fight.[2] In a contest between good and evil who could doubt that victory would be speedy ? " Cordially united with France," said a writer in *The Quarterly*, " and engaged in a righteous contest, we have little to dread from a Power which has added to the other elements of its weakness by the injustice of its cause." [3] But mere defeat of the Tsar was insufficient : the war was one to free Europe. For this purpose would it not be better to declare war on Austria too ? Kossuth was touring the country, keeping fresh the memory of Austrian and Russian intervention in 1849 and reiterating that now was the time to give the help that we failed to offer then. " The war," he declared in July, " is a logical necessity. In vain Cabinet diplomacy strains every nerve to tear from the lips of oppressed nations the ripe fruit of long-cherished hopes. The force of events will baffle their tricks." . . . Poland, Hungary, and Italy would now attain their freedom. " You failed," he told his English audiences, " to aid Hungary when the Tsar first struck down her young Republic, and now you have to pay for it with your blood in streams and your money by millions." Could we think of obtaining an alliance with Austria in a war to crush Russia ? The

---

[1] *A Knouting for the Tsar.* Words on the battles of Inkerman, Balaclava, and Alva, by a Soldier, 1855.

[2] Cp. *Hurrah for Old England and Charley Napier*, by T. Pearce, and accounts in all the papers of the farewell banquet to Sir Charles Napier, 12/3/54.

[3] Vol. 94, 301. For a terribly sanguine article about the war vide *M.P.*, 7/2/54.

answer was clear : " Crush both " came from every part of the crowd.[1] Exactly how this was to be done was for the most part undecided. But Russia must be permanently crippled. Details were supplied by pamphleteers. " The object of the present war," one wrote, " is the establishment of the peace and security of Europe on a solid and permanent foundation." The allies must " reduce the material power of Russia in such a manner as to preclude the possibility of her continuing schemes of aggrandizement " ; much of her territory—the Crimea, Bessarabia, and Finland—was wrongfully acquired and must be taken away. Above all, Poland must again become an independent kingdom.

[1] Kossuth's speech on June 5, 1854. Cp. also *D. N.*, 27/2/54— article on the danger of ruining the war for Poland, Hungary, and Italy if an alliance was made with Austria. The broadside, *Oh ! Lovely Albert !* (three verses of which are quoted, Strachey, 177–8) illustrates the assumption that war with Russia must also involve hostility to all German-speaking races.

> Bad luck they say, both night and day
>   To the Cobugs and the humbugs,
> The Witermbugs and Scarembugs,
>   And all the German horserugs :
> And the old bug of Aberdeen,
>   The Peterbugs and Prussians,
> May Providence protect the Turks,
>   And massacre the Russians.
>
> Let France and England go to work,
>   Shun Austrians and Prussians,
> Assist the poor and injured Turks,
>   And smother all the Russians ;
> Chain up the bear and make him stare,
>   And so keep my Davy,
> We'll sing Old England three time three,
>   The Army and the Navy.
>
> *Chorus.*
> I will tell thee AL, we never shall,
>   Although you played the deuce then,
> Allow the Turks to be run down
>   By the dirty, greasy Russians.

Would not the Duke of Cambridge be the "most desirable personage to fill the throne of Poland?" A "large indemnity" was to be extracted from Russia, and the allies were to see that her Government was reformed and her administrative system overhauled.[1]

While this vivid picture of a struggle for liberty prevailed, all arguments against the war necessarily seemed cowardly. It became a common method of displaying patriotism to write letters to the papers or publish pamphlets denouncing the " peacemongers." Neither Bright nor Cobden had shrunk from stating their opinions. Bright's position, stated in the House of Commons before the declaration of war, was summarized in his letter to Mr. Absalom Watkin and printed in *The Times* of November 3, 1854. He opposed the war on three main grounds.[2] The first was that after the Vienna Note the allies had had no further obligation to support Turkey. We were fighting for a country which had refused our mediation against a country which had accepted our terms. " At this moment *England is engaged in a murderous warfare with Russia, although the Russian Government accepted her own terms of peace* and has been willing to accept them in the sense of England's own interpretation of them since they were offered : and at the same time England is allied *with Turkey, whose Government rejected the award of England, and who entered into the war in opposition to the advice of England.* Surely, when the Vienna Note was accepted by Russia, the Turks should have been prevented from going to war, or should have been allowed to go to war at their own risk."

[1] Krasinski, a Polish refugee in England.
[2] Bright never opposed the Crimean War on the Quaker ground that war is wrong under all circumstances.

In the second place he argued that if we were
to intervene at all in the East it should be in favour
of Russia, however bad her Government, rather
than for Turkey, the horror of whose administration
could not be surpassed. " We are not only at
war with Russia, but with all the Christian population of the Turkish Empire, and we are building
up our Eastern policy on a false foundation—
namely, on the perpetual maintenance of the most
immoral and filthy of all despotisms, over one of
the fairest portions of the earth, which it has
desolated, and over a population it has degraded
but has not been able to destroy. . . . The danger
of Russian power was a phantom ; the necessity
of permanently upholding the Mahometan rule in
Europe an absurdity. Our love for civilization,
when we subject the Greeks and Christians to the
Turks, is a sham ; and our sacrifices for freedom
when working out the behests of the Emperor of
the French and coaxing Austria to help us is a
pitiful imposture.

" The evils of non-intervention were remote and
vague, and could neither be weighed nor described
in any accurate terms. The good we can judge
something of already by estimating the cost of a
contrary policy. And what is the cost ? War in
the north (Baltic) and south of Europe, threatening
to involve every country of Europe. Money, perhaps fifty millions sterling in the course of expenditure by this country alone, to be raised from the
taxes of people whose extrication from ignorance
and poverty can only be hoped for from the
continuance of peace. The disturbance of trade
throughout the world, the derangement of monetary
affairs, and difficulties and ruin to thousands of
families. Another year of high prices of food,
notwithstanding a full harvest in England, chiefly

because war interferes with imports, and we have declared our principal food-growers to be our enemies. The loss of life to an enormous extent. Many thousands of our own countrymen have already perished of pestilence in the field and hundreds, perhaps thousands, of English families will be plunged into sorrow, as a part of the penalty to be paid for the folly of the nation and its rulers.

" When the time comes for the ' inquisition of blood,' who shall answer for these things ? You have read the tidings from the Crimea ; you have perhaps shuddered at the slaughter ; you remember the terrific picture—I speak not of the battle and of the charge and the tumultuous excitement of the conflict, but of the field after the battle— Russians in their frenzy or their terror shooting Englishmen who would have offered them water to quench their agony of thirst ; Englishmen, in crowds, rifling the pockets of the men they had slain or wounded, taking their few shillings or roubles, and discovering among the plunder of the stiffening corpses images of the ' Virgin and the Child.' You have read this and your imagination has followed the fearful details. This is war— every crime human nature can commit or imagine, every horror it can perpetrate or suffer ; and this it is which our Christian Government recklessly plunges into, and which so many of our countrymen at this minute think it patriotic to applaud."

In the winter that followed, when *The Times* was day by day pouring out its terrible story of disease, misery, and incompetence in the Crimea, when it had become obvious that the war would not benefit Poland or Hungary, and that Russia was as capable of dull resistance to the invader as she had been in the days of Napoleon, the

words of Bright were here and there recalled.[1]
But for the moment every argument that Bright
used was instinctively adapted to the popular
image and became an argument for more active
hostilities.

In the first place, his opponents retorted, the
Vienna Note ought never to have been offered to
Turkey. Only a weak or treacherous Government
would have " played the Tsar's game " by offering
him terms that he was willing to accept. His
immediate compliance with the terms proved that
they suited his purpose in dismembering Turkey.
Bright's second argument seemed at first more
forcible. Turkish rule of Christian minorities had
long troubled religious persons. Now, however,
when they felt that the war was for civilization,
it was also clear that in some way or other it must
be for Christianity. In the first place, since Turkey
was said to be tolerant and Russia notoriously
oppressed all forms of Christianity except her own,
the war was for the benefit of Christians. We
were, therefore, said *The Quarterly Review*, " fighting
not for Islam but for Christianity." [2] Moreover,
the war was a war for justice. " Justice," said Mr.
Langford in an answer to John Bright, " is another
word for Christianity ; therefore we were fighting

---

[1] A number of pamphlets of 1855 confess agreement with Bright
and occasionally even conversion by him. In the early part of 1854
I have only seen two pamphlets against the war, one being written
by a Russian. For examples of the effect of Bright's argument
when facts had broken down the picture of 1854, *Diplomatic
Mystifications and Popular Credulity*, 1855 ; *War Unmasked*, by
an ex-M.P. ; *History of the Origin of the War with Russia*, 1855 ;
Is the War Just ? Letter to Rt. Hon. Viscount Palmerston, 1855 ;
*Inquiry into the Alleged Justice and Necessity of the War with
Russia, by a Land-owner*, 1855. Against the war in 1854 are :
A Word to the British Public ; An Appeal on the Eastern Question,
by a Russian.

[2] March 1854, 556-8.

for Christianity." [1] But there were more profound arguments than this. Religious teachers of many shades of faith declared that the war was sent by God and would call forth the slumbering virtue in men who were enervated by the effeminate habits of peace. The nations of the world, said one writer, have been unwilling to engage in this war, " yet God as Judge is standing at the door of battle and they go in against their wills." Our sin had necessitated the war. Yet " every war is a war of principles " and God had chosen to make our punishment the instrument of his Providence. Victory was certain, for God and the allied troops were acting together. " In a religious point of view the means and agencies now employed with such others as may reasonably be expected to spring up out of an advancing state of things, combined with the official agency of the Holy Ghost, seem to me amply sufficient for affecting a great and glorious change in the present evil world." [2]

A further hope arose. Could it be that the battle with the evil power of Russia was the final struggle destined by divine prophecy to take place before the Second Coming? The Rev. Archibald Boyd told the Church of England Reading Association that he found many signs that this was the case. Did we not know that " the drying up of the Euphrates " was to be the conclusion of a great prophetic period? Was Turkey perhaps destined to be the last great convert to Christ before the final catastrophe! [3]

" Possibly, in the convulsions which changes so

[1] Langford.
[2] Palmer. The same writer, referring to the death of the Tsar, wrote : " The suggestive remark of the Saviour naturally comes to one's recollection : ' I beheld Satan as lightning fall from Heaven.' "
[3] Boyd.

momentous and so pregnant with strife must produce, there will be found the commencement of that state of universal disturbance which is to herald and introduce the advent of the Son of Man." Mr. Boyd, however, was a little doubtful ; it would be safer at present to preserve the Ottoman Empire by the usual methods until we knew more certainly that worldly efforts were no longer necessary. The Vicar of Kenilworth had no doubt that the last trump would follow the last British victory. " It may be," he said, " in the Providence of God, as I firmly believe, that our beloved country is destined to be a great instrument in preparing the world for that unspeakably glorious event." [1]

More cautious ministers of many shades of faith, who did not identify the Crimean War with Armaggedon, vehemently controverted Bright's view that war was harmful to the national character. Among the less orthodox Christians, James Martineau declared that England must accept the war as a sacred trust to vindicate " the common and universal law of God," which had " been offended," and would be delayed by the advance of Russian despotism.[2] Dr. Dale of Birmingham rejoiced that the nation had shown itself capable of sacrifice for unselfish ends, that we were fighting on behalf of Hungary and Poland, and not to extend our commerce or territory, but for the sake of justice, mercy, and truth. Such a war would bring forth " the most heroic and Christian virtues " in every citizen.[3]

In the Anglican Church the same assurance prevailed. At first, it is true, Charles Kingsley and Frederick Denison Maurice found the war puzzling. Both, however, quickly learnt to see in it the guiding hand of God and to realize that " awful as war is " its results were " more good

[1] Kenilworth, 1855.   [2] Drummond, i. 270.   [3] Dale, 130.

THE EVE OF WAR

than evil." Kingsley felt that it was his task to help the English soldier to realize that he was "fighting on God's side," and wrote a pamphlet entitled *Brave Words to Brave Soldiers* to emphasize this aspect of the war. He said: "A soldier wants a military and corporate and national religion, and that is what I fear he has yet to get and what I tried to give him in my tract. That is what Cromwell's Ironsides had, and by it they conquered. This is what the Elizabethans had up to the Armada, and by it they conquered."[1] During the first year of the war he set himself to portray the religion of the Elizabethans in *Westward Ho!* and, with an ingenuous sincerity which schoolboys have always found delightful, contrived to endow the teaching of the Gospels with something of his own adventurous spirit. Maurice wrote, congratulating him on the idea of his Elizabethan novel, but reminding him that in his preaching, too, he must supply the "burning fire" of which the Church stood in need.

"I do hope something from the war," he wrote, "chiefly as a sign of what God is doing. It is more like the commencement of a battle between God in His Absoluteness and the Tsar in his than 1848 was, though that might take a more agreeable and popular form. I begin to understand a little better why our sympathies with Greece and even Italy were so violently stifled. Something better is to come for both than the pirates and brigands could get for them."

And later he found that the "war has brought more good, with all its misery, than I could have dreamed. I am sure there is something more like a national heart of godliness amongst us than I have had any experience of in my day. The

[1] Kingsley, i. 334-5 ; Maurice, ii. 240-51.

Let it flame or fade, and the war roll down like a wind
We have proved we have hearts in a cause, we are noble still,
And myself have awaked, as it seems, to the better mind;
It is better to fight for the good than to rail at the ill;
I have felt with my native land, I am one with my kind,
I embrace the purpose of God, and the doom assign'd. [1]

There was no cause for fear. Englishmen were noble still. Before them was a vision of triumphant wrong, and, moved by a disinterested and generous passion, they welcomed the opportunity of fighting for the right. The vision, however, bore little or no relation to the facts, and it is perhaps a little ironical that the chivalrous desire to aid the oppressed against the tyrant should find its outlet in a war on behalf of Turkey. " What Englishmen condemn," says Mr. Simpson, " is almost always worthy of condemnation—if only it has happened." [2]

Nor had " the long, long canker of peace " destroyed English courage and determination. In the winter of 1854 there was opportunity for both. The Crimean campaign showed that heroic obedience was a quality which the British soldier still possessed, however incompetent his commanders, and Lord Tennyson was soon provided with material for another poem. It also revealed that the whole system of English administration was in the hands of " antiquated imbecility." An indignant public discovered " the incompetency, lethargy, aristocratic hauteur, official indifference, favour, routine, perverseness, and stupidity which revel and riot in the camp before Sevastopol." [3] The war was the price which England paid for the reform of some of these defects. In exposing them the race of war correspondents was born, and

[1] "Maud," 1854.   [2] Simpson, 166 n.
[3] Times, 23/12/54; quoted Trevelyan, G. M., 236.

The Times, best served by William Howard Russell, reached the summit of its glory. At the same time a new race of women arose. Indeed, but for the horrors of Scutari, Florence Nightingale might have died unknown and England have ignored the most remarkable of her eminent Victorians. So the British character once more triumphed, though, to be sure, the triumph has had to be repeated on several subsequent occasions.

Outside England the results of the war were equally unexpected. Only five years after peace had been made, *The Times* admitted that British idealism had been misplaced :

" We must frankly own that we feel somewhat more free to act like men and Christians than we could five years ago. That ill-starred war, those half-million of British, French, and Russian men left in the Crimea, those two hundred millions of money wasted in the worst of all ways, have discharged to the last iota all the debt of Christian Europe to Turkey. Never was so great an effort made for so worthless an object. It is with no small reluctance that we admit a gigantic effort and an infinite sacrifice to have been made in vain." Historians have, for the most part, accepted this verdict. Those who have defended the war have usually done so on the ground that it restored the Balance of Power and aided in the struggle for national freedom.

Russian strength, however, always greater in defence than attack, was not long crippled, and in fifteen years her fleet was again dominant in the Black Sea. A few years later, indeed, Mr. Disraeli thought it again necessary to fight the tyrant, while Mr. Gladstone, strangely enough, thought that the liberty of Turkey to massacre Bulgarians had been bought at too high a price *of British Foreign Policy.*[1] He has brought together the political results of the war with admirable clarity, and it seems desirable to consider whether they form an adequate vindication of the reliability of British public opinion.

In the first place, Mr. Reddaway seems to be of the opinion that, in general, the instinctive morality of the British public, unspoilt by too much knowledge of the facts, may be trusted to guide the national foreign policy. Lord Palmerston and the " overwhelming majority of the nation," whom he represented, were right. Any other policy on England's part—whether it was one of isolation, adjournment, or joint-partition of Turkey— would, he thinks, have been dishonourable to England and dangerous to the liberties of Europe. " It was at bottom the defence of popular liberty against the menacing reaction, incarnate and triumphant in the Tsar, that brought Great Britain into the field. Not for the last time, the nation, rendered vocal by its Press, pronounced a clearer judgment than its statesmen upon the rights and wrongs of humanity." " For Russia recognized no limits to its destiny," and without the war the Baltic States would have been swiftly comprised within the Empire of the Tsar. " Roumania and Bulgaria at least owe their ultimate independence to the compulsory quiescence of Russia, and the Balkan League, then as little dreamed of as the German Empire, is the offspring of the Congress of Paris." " Henceforward Russia might recover Bessarabia and the Black Sea, but hardly control the Eastern Question. A generation later it could be laid down that collective authority on the part of the Powers to regulate the disintegration of Turkey had been exercised systematically since 1856."

To this vindication of the rights of national freedom he adds that, though the Crimean War did not knit "a perfect union of hearts between the French and British peoples," their " common efforts in an unselfish cause weakened their old estrangement," and apparently prevented Napoleon from invading the " almost defenceless shores of England." Whereas before the war England had been of no account in Europe, " no one could deny that at its close a far more salutary distribution of power prevailed." " On the Continent, the proof that Great Britain both could and might intervene effectively to support a principle gave her some years of high prestige. To this, in no small degree, Italy owes her freedom. At home, on the other hand, the war left a legacy of distaste for Continental adventure which for nearly sixty years set free the surplus energies of Great

[1] Vol. ii. chap. viii.

Britain to be exercised across the ocean." "Upon Russia the blindfold surgery of the allies conferred the benefits which they had vainly hoped that Turkey would receive. The military autocracy confessed its failure, and for nearly a decade Western institutions were showered upon the people." And, may we not add, thus directly contributed to the Bolshevik Revolution of 1917?

Now English public opinion had certainly not anticipated these results and yet, apparently, it is vindicated by them. Instinctive morality, when it demands war against a tyrant, somehow leads to the greatest happiness of the greatest number. Here is a mystic union between the intuitionist and the utilitarian. Yet there are surely difficulties in accepting the usual criteria of either. Tyrants change and time has a curiously rapid way of altering our judgments about the Balance of Power and the right people to choose as our friends. And if we are to look at the indirect results of the war where, amid the vast congeries of events, are we to begin and where end? Would it not be wiser, after all, to leave the results unexamined, and to cleave exclusively to the position that we need must fight the evil when we see it?

In the first place we may admit that the war added for a time to British "prestige" and tended to direct British energies abroad. We might go further. There is no doubt that as a result of Palmerston's victory over Cobdenism in England the British people more readily learnt that it was at once their gain and their duty to increase their power by interfering in the affairs of such other peoples as could not easily retaliate. This policy has not, however, led them either to permanent friendship with France nor again to the eternal hostility with Russia, which seems to be suggested. In fact, there have been noticeable fluctuations in the alliances of nations "united for common efforts in unselfish causes."

Moreover, the Balance of Power was but precariously established. The check to Russian ambition was a slight one. At most, it seems, we can claim that, as a result of the war, the "collective authority of the Powers" has since agreed to "regulate the disintegration of Turkey." It was, after all, the Tsar who first suggested this—he proposed that England should take Egypt—and it is perhaps a little curious to fight a war to prevent a certain policy and then to justify the war afterwards on the grounds that, as one of its results, that very policy has since proved successful. The disintegration of Turkey is, however, still incomplete owing to the

Escott.—Masters of English Journalism. By T. H. S. Escott. 1911.

Fawcett.—Life of Sir William Molesworth. By Mrs. Fawcett. 2 vols. 1901.

Fonblanque.—Life and Labours of Albany Fonblanque. By Edward Barrington. 1874.

Fox-Bourne.—English Newspapers. By H. R. Fox-Bourne. 2 vols. 1887.

Froude.—My Relations with Carlyle. By J. A. Froude. 2 vols. 1890.

Gardiner.—Life of Sir William Harcourt. By A. G. Gardiner. 2 vols. 1923.

Glenesk.—Lord Glenesk and *The Morning Post.* By Reginald Lucas. 1910.

Grant.—The Newspaper Press : its Origin and Present Position. 3 vols. 1871.

Granville.—Life of the Second Earl Granville. By Lord E. Fitzmaurice. 2 vols. 1905.

Greville.—A Journal of the Reign of Queen Victoria. By Charles Greville. Edited by Henry Reeve. 8 vols. 1888.

Hansard.

Hayward.—The Correspondence of Abraham Hayward from 1834–84. Edited by Henry E. Carlisle. 2 vols. 1886.

Henry Greville.—Leaves from the Diary of Henry Greville, 1801–72. Edited by Viscountess Enfield. 4 vols. 1883–1905.

Hobson.—Richard Cobden. The International Man. By J. A. Hobson. 1918.

Holyoake.—Sixty Years of an Agitator's Life, 1830–90. By G. Jacob Holyoake. 2 vols. 1892.

Kinglake.—The Invasion of the Crimea. By A. W. Kinglake. 9 vols. Cabinet Edition. 1878.

Kingsley.—Letters and Memories of the Life of Charles Kingsley. Edited by his wife. 2 vols. 1877.

Lane Poole.—The Life of Stratford-Canning. By Stanley Lane Poole. 2 vols. 1888.

Layard.—Autobiography and Letters of Sir Henry Layard. 2 vols. 1903.

Letters.—The Letters of Queen Victoria. 3 vols. 1908.

Lewis.—The Letters of Sir George Cornwall Lewis. 1890.

Loftus.—Reminiscences of Augustus Loftus, 1837–62. 1st Series. 2 volumes. 1892.

Lytton.—Life of Edward Bulwer, First Lord Lytton. By his grandson, the Earl of Lytton. 2 vols. 1913.

MACKAY.—Through the Long Day. By Charles Mackay. 2 vols. 1887.

MALMESBURY.—Memoirs of an ex-Minister. An Autobiography. By the Earl of Malmesbury. 2 vols. 1884.

MARTIN.—The Life of H.R.H. The Prince Consort. By Sir Theodore Martin. 5 vols. 1880.

MAURICE.—The Life of Frederick Denison Maurice, chiefly told in his Letters. Edited by his son. 2 vols. 1884.

MAXWELL.—Life of the Fourth Earl of Clarendon. By Sir Herbert Maxwell. 2 vols. 1913.

MIALL.—Edward Miall. By his son. 1884.

MORLEY, COBDEN.—The Life of Richard Cobden. By John Morley. 2 vols. (Eversley Edition).

MORLEY, GLADSTONE.—The Life of William Ewart Gladstone. By John Morley. 3 vols. 1903.

OLIPHANT.—Memories of the Life of Laurence Oliphant and of Alice Oliphant, his Wife. 1891.

PARKER.—The Life and Letters of Sir James Graham, 1792–1861. By Charles Stuart Parker. 2 vols. 1907.

REEVE.—Memoirs of the Life and Correspondence of Henry Reeve. By John Knox Laughton. 2 vols. 1898.

REID.—The Life, Letters and Friendships of Richard Monckton Milnes, First Lord Houghton. By T. Wemyss Reid. 2 vols. 1890.

RICHARD.—Memoirs of Joseph Sturge. By Henry Richard. 1864.

ROBINSON.—Fifty Years of Fleet Street. By Sir John Robinson. 1904.

RUSSELL.—Recollections of John, Earl Russell. 1813–73.

SCHIEMANN.—Geschichte Russlands unter Nikolaus I. By T. Schiemann. 4 vols. Berlin. 1904.

SIMPSON.—Louis Napoleon and the Recovery of France, 1848–56. By F. A. Simpson. 1923.

SPROXTON.—Palmerston and the Hungarian Revolution. By Charles Sproxton. 1919.

STANMORE.—Life of Lord Aberdeen. By Lord Stanmore. 1893.

STANMORE, SIDNEY HERBERT.—A Memoir of Sidney Herbert. By Lord Stanmore. 2 vols. 1906.

STOCKMAR.—Memoirs of Baron Stockmar. By his son. 2 vols. (English Edition. 1872.)

STRACHEY.—Queen Victoria. By Lytton Strachey. 1921.

TAYLOR.—Correspondence of Sir Henry Taylor. Edited by Edward Dowden. 1888.

TREVELYAN, G. M.—Life of John Bright. By George Macaulay Trevelyan. 1913.

TREVELYAN, G. O.—Life and Letters of Lord Macaulay. By Sir G. O. Trevelyan. 2 vols.

URQUHART.—David Urquhart. By Gertrude Robinson. 1920.

VITZTHUM.—St. Petersburg and London in the years 1852–64. Reminiscences of Count Frederick Vitzthum von Eckstaedt. Edited by Henry Reeve. 1887.

WALPOLE.—Life of Lord John Russell. By Sir Spencer Walpole. 2 vols. 1889.

WHEELER.—Letters of Walter Savage Landor. Private and Public. Edited by Stephen Wheeler. 1899.

NEWSPAPERS AND PERIODICALS.

Bell's Life (Bell's).
Blackwood's Magazine (Blackwood's).
The Daily News (D.N.).
The Edinburgh Review (Edinburgh).
The Examiner.
Frazer's Magazine (Frazer's).
The Globe.
The Guardian.
The Herald of Peace.
The Illustrated London News.
John Bull.
The Manchester Guardian (M.G.).
The Morning Advertiser (M.A.).
The Morning Chronicle (M.C.).
The Morning Herald (M.H.).
The Morning Post (M.P.).
The Press.
Punch.
The Quarterly Review (Quarterly).
Reynolds's Weekly (Reynolds's).
The Russian Review.
The Spectator.
The Standard.
The Times.
The Weekly Despatch.
The Westminster Review (Westminster).

BROADSIDES AND SONGS (from the British Museum).

Cardinal Wiseman. Song by W. Everson. 1850.
Chobham Camp. 1853.
England and Napoleon. 1852.
Lovely Albert ! 1854.
The Crystal Palace. 1851.
War Verses. By various authors. 1853–6.

PAMPHLETS.

A Few Kind Words and Practical Hints to Young Soldiers. By an Officer. 1854.

AIRPLAY, F.—Prince Albert. Why is he Unpopular ? 1854.

A Knouting for the Tsar. Words on the Battles of Inkerman, Balaclava, and Alva. By a Soldier. 1855.

Another Note on the Eastern Question, not by Authority but by the Author. December 1853.

An Appeal on the Eastern Question. By a Russian. 1854.

APPLETON, LEWIS.—The Wars of Queen Victoria's Reign (1837–87).

Authentic Report of Kossuth's Speeches on the War in the East and the Alliance with Austria. 1854.

BOYD.—Turkey and the Turks. (Lecture to the Church of England Reading Association.) By Rev. Archibald Boyd. December 1853.

COBDEN, RICHARD.—1792 and 1853 in Three Letters. January 1853.

The Three Panics. An Historical Episode. 1862.

CONINGHAM, W.—Lord Palmerston and Prince Albert. (Published January 1854.)

Diplomatic Mystifications and Popular Credulity. 1855.

FERGUSON, JAMES.—The Perils of Portsmouth. 1852.

History of the Origin of the War from Parliamentary Documents. 1855.

Inquiry into the Alleged Justice and Necessity of the War. with Russia. 1855.

Is the War Just? A letter to the Rt. Hon. Viscount Palmerston, 1855.

KENILWORTH.—A New Year's Address (1855). By the Vicar of Kenilworth.

KINGSLEY.—Brave Words to Brave Soldiers. By the Rev. Charles Kingsley. 1854.

KRASINSKI.—Russia and Europe; or the Probable Consequences of the Present War. By Count Valerian Krasinski. 1854.

LANGFORD, J. A.—War with Russia: its Origin and Cause. A reply to the letter of John Bright. 1855.

LISTER, HENRY.—War with Russia: England's Duties and Interests in the East. 1854.

LUSHINGTON, HENRY.—La Nation Boutiquière. 1855.

LUSHINGTON, FRANKLIN.—Points of War. 1854.

MACFARLINE, CHARLES.—Kismet; or the Doom of Turkey. 1853.

MARX, KARL.—The Eastern Question. A reprint of letters to the New York Tribune, 1853–6. By Karl Marx. Edited by E. M. Aveling and E. Aveling. 1897.

The Story of Lord Palmerston. By Karl Marx. Edited by E. M. Aveling. 1899.

" Nemo."—A Word to the British Public before Entering into
Hostilities with Russia. 1854.

OLIPHANT, LAURENCE.—On the Shores of the Black Sea. 1853.

Observations on the Character and Conduct of the Prince
Consort. Anonymous. 1854(?).

" Pacificus."—One Word for Russia and Two for Ourselves. 1853.

PALMER, W.—The Present Struggle ; or Calm Reflections on
the Retributive Character of War, the Moral Government
of God, etc. By Rev. William Palmer. 1855.

Peace or War ? A letter to the Rt. Hon. the Earl of Aberdeen. 1854.

PEARCE, T.—Hurrah for Old England and Charley Napier.
1854.

Prince Albert. Anonymous. 1854.

Prince Albert's Defence. Anonymous. 1854.

Remarks on the Present Aspect of the Turkish Question.
By a Member of the University of Oxford. 1853.

SMITH, WILLIAM ADAM.—" A Last Appeal. War or Peace ?
1854.

The Powers of Europe and the World's Great Quarrel, or
the Philosophy and Morality of the Present War.

URQUHART, DAVID.—Recent Events in the East. 1854.

Progress of Russia in the West, North and South. 1853.

Materials for the True History of Lord Palmerston. 1866.

The Queen and the Premier (Viscount Palmerston). A
Statement of their Struggle and its Results. By D.
Urquhart. 1857.

" Veritas." Partition of Turkey, an Indispensable Feature of
the Present Political Crisis." 1853.

CONTEMPORARY LITERATURE.

KINGSLEY.—Westward Ho ! By Charles Kingsley. 1854.

MEREDITH.—Beauchamp's Career. By George Meredith. 1876.

TENNYSON.—Locksley Hall. 1842.

Ode on the Death of the Duke of Wellington. 1852.
Maud. 1854.

The Charge of the Light Brigade. 1855.

INDEX

Aberdeen, Earl of, 25, 53 ; relations with Tsar, 29–30 ; regrets Olmütz, 36–7 158, 223 ; forms Cabinet, 78 *et seq.* ; character as leader, 80–1 ; pacific intentions, 83 ; relations with Delane and the Press, 92, 99, 101–2, 123, 213. Attitude to " Sick man," 105, 113, 138 ; to Stratford, 107, 139 ; to Russia, 111–16 ; to public opinion, 116–17, 142 ; to Vienna Note, 149 ; to Peace Conference, 192. Attacked in Press, 124 *et seq.*, 152 *et seq.* ; by Urquhart, 142 ; by " Plain Speech," 209. Cabinet difficulties and hesitations, 134–5, 157, 159–60, 164 *et seq.*, relations with Palmerston, 173–82; correspondence with Queen, 167, 210 *et seq.*, 217 ; desire to resign, 220 ; regrets war, 221–3.

Adrianople, Treaty of, 33 *n.*, 35, 127.

Albert, Prince, 53, 81 *n.*, 142, 161, 167 ; relations with Palmerston 64, 172–6, 201 ; attacked, 203–14.

America, 186.

Anti-Corn Law League, 46–7.

Argyll, Duke of, 83, 113, 157, 163–4, 168, 218–19.

Austria, opinion in England towards alliance with, 24, 34 *et seq.*, 41, 113, 121, 129, 132, 152, 186, 190, 216–17, 231 ; attitude to refugees, 50–1, 120 ; result of the war on, 244, 248.

Bagehot, Walter, cited, 86.

Baldwin, Edward, 98 *n.*

Barnes, John, 87.

Belgium, 117.

Bentham, *Public Opinion Tribunal*, 16–18 ; free Press, 85.

Bell's Life, 49, 126–7, 146, 200, 206.

Besika Bay, 82, 142

Bismarck, 244.

Black, John, 92 *n.*

Borneo, " Rajah " Brooke in, 49.

Borthwick, Algernon, 96, 198, *vide The Morning Post.*

Borthwick, Peter, 95, 97.

Bosnia, 104, 129.

Boyd, Rev. Archibald, 237.

Bright, John, 45, 46, 48, 57, 191, 221 *n.*, 223–5, 227, 233–6, 240

Brooke, " Rajah," 49.

Brougham, Lord, 86 *n.*

Brown, General, 208.

Brunmow, Baron, 31, 105, 162.

Bulgaria, 244, 246.

Buol, Count, 190 *n.*, 193.

Burke, Edmund, on French Revolution, 19.

Cambridge, Duke of, 233.

Canning, George, 54, 85.

Carlyle, Thomas, 21, 226.

Cavour, Count, 244.

Cecil, Algernon, cited, 110.

Channel Islands, 117.

Charleton, Robert, 227 *n.*

Cherbourg, 74.

Chester, Meeting at, 185.

Chobham Camp, 104.

Clanricarde, Lord, 145.

Clarendon, Lady, 221.

Clarendon, Lord, 41, 83, 92, 109, 111, 115–17, 124 *et seq.*, 128, 131–2, 135 *et seq.*, 144–7, 155–7, 161–8, 170, 183, 192, 217, 221.

Cobbett, William, 85.

Cobden, Richard, 46–51, 57, 83, 119, 136, 227, 233, 240.

Coningham, William, 207.

Constantinople, 37, 105, 125, 130, 133, 138, 142, 152, 216.

Cook, J. D., 93, 196.

Cowley, Lord, 40, 138–9.

Cranworth, Lord Chancellor, 157.

Crimean War, Origins of, 25 *et seq.*; negotiations leading to, 28 *et seq.*; results of, 243–8.

17

Printed in Great Britain by
UNWIN BROTHERS, LIMITED
LONDON AND WOKING